134 COPYCAT RECIPES THAT TRULY DEL

Do you ever want to treat yourself to a drive-thru classic but don't f
Have a craving for a restaurant favorite, but once you get the bill, yc
your budget intact from the comfort of home by preparing your most-loved restaurant dishes
yourself! Simply turn to this fabulous collection of mouthwatering favorites from fast-food hot
spots, coffee shops and eateries that are popular from coast to coast.

With the recipes included here, it's a snap to re-create all of the main courses, appetizers and
desserts you could previously enjoy only while out to eat. Inspired by Starbucks, Cheesecake
Factory, Red Lobster, Boston Market, Burger King,
Chipotle, P.F. Chang's, Olive Garden, KFC and other
famous restaurants, these secret recipes satisfy
your hunger as well as your wallet.

LOOK INSIDE TO FIND THE TASTIEST DISHES

Copycat Entrees: Forget the take-out menu. Fried
chicken dinners, juicy burgers and shrimp specialties
are here to jazz up mealtime!

Eye-Opening Breakfasts: Start the day right—without
leaving home! From bagels and waffles to smoothies
and granola bars, these recipes promise to awaken
you *and* your taste buds.

Coffee Shop Favorites: Need your daily latte fix?
Spend your time and cash wisely by making coffee
house specialties at home.

Best Appetizers Ever: From mozzarella sticks to pot
stickers, these snacks are perfect for parties.

Specialty Soups, Salads & Sandwiches: Mix and match
these craveworthy menu staples for a marvelous
lunch or light dinner.

Double-Take Desserts: Satisfy your sweet tooth with
an impressive duplicate of a restaurant fave.

Not only does every recipe include a complete set of
nutrition facts, but each dish was tested and approved
at the *Taste of Home* Test Kitchen. Whipping up an
impressive copycat surprise has never been easier,
tastier or more affordable! Best of all, you can relish
these bites from the comfort of your very own home.

TABLE OF CONTENTS

MORE WAYS TO CONNECT WITH US:

Taste of Home

COPYCAT
FAVORITES

TASTE OF HOME BOOKS • RDA ENTHUSIAST BRANDS, LLC • MILWAUKEE, WI

© 2023 RDA Enthusiast Brands, LLC.
1610 N. 2nd St., Suite 102,
Milwaukee WI 53212-3906
All rights reserved. Taste of Home is a
registered trademark of RDA Enthusiast
Brands, LLC.

Printed in USA
10 9 8 7 6 5 4 3 2 1

Taste of Home Copycat Favorites
ISBN: 978-1-62145-933-0

Pictured on front cover:
Copycat Red Lobster Cheddar Bay
Biscuits, p. 214

Pictured on back cover:
Copycat Fried Chicken Sandwich, p. 110;
Pink Drink, p. 46; Copycat Nothing Bundt
Cake, p. 235; Copycat Southwest Chicken
Salad, p. 94

**Taste of Home Copycat
Restaurant Favorites**
ISBN: 978-1-62145-961-3

Pictured on front cover:
Copycat Fried Chicken Sandwich,
p. 110; Copycat Red Lobster Cheddar Bay
Biscuits, p. 214; Homemade Oreo Cookies,
p. 240; Copycat Southwest Chicken Salad,
p. 94

Pictured on back cover:
Freezer Breakfast Sandwiches, p. 34;
Pink Drink, p. 46; Copycat Nothing Bundt
Cake, p. 235; Copycat Mac & Cheese,
p. 181

Pictured on title page:
Pork & Chive Pot Stickers, p. 65 ;
Copycat Chick-Fil-A Sauce, p. 209;
Copycat Celebration Cheesecake, p. 228;
White Cheese Dip, p. 61

Chief Content Officer, Home & Garden:
Jeanne Sidner
Content Director: Mark Hagen
Creative Director: Raeann Thompson
Senior Art Director: Courtney Lovetere
Senior Designer: Jazmin Delgado
Designer: Carrie Peterson
Editor: Sara Strauss
Deputy Editor, Copy Desk: Dulcie Shoener

Cover Photography:
Photographer: Mark Derse
Set Stylist: Stacey Genaw
Food Stylist: Josh Rink

**INSPIRED BY
DISNEYLAND THEME PARK®**
DOLE WHIP, P. 198

EYE-OPENING BREAKFASTS

Stash some cash by whipping up a drive-thru favorite at home. It's easy with these early-morning copycat recipes.

FRENCH TOAST STICKS

Keep these French toast sticks in the freezer for an instant filling breakfast.
Their convenient size makes them ideal for a breakfast buffet.
—Taste of Home *Test Kitchen*

PREP: 20 MIN. + FREEZING • **BAKE:** 20 MIN. • **MAKES:** 1½ DOZEN

6 slices day-old Texas toast
4 large eggs
1 cup 2% milk
2 Tbsp. sugar
1 tsp. vanilla extract
¼ to ½ tsp. ground cinnamon
1 cup crushed cornflakes,
   optional
   Confectioners' sugar, optional
   Maple syrup

1. Cut each piece of bread into thirds; place in a single layer in an ungreased 13x9-in. dish. In a large bowl, whisk the eggs, milk, sugar, vanilla and cinnamon. Pour over bread; soak for 2 minutes, turning once. If desired, coat bread with cornflake crumbs on all sides.

2. Place in a greased 15x10x1-in. baking pan. Freeze until firm, about 45 minutes. Transfer to an airtight freezer container and store in the freezer.

3. Place desired number of frozen sticks on a greased baking sheet. Bake at 425° for 8 minutes. Turn; bake 10-12 minutes longer or until golden brown. Sprinkle with confectioners' sugar if desired. Serve with syrup.

3 sticks: 183 cal., 6g fat (2g sat. fat), 145mg chol., 251mg sod., 24g carb. (8g sugars, 1g fiber), 8g pro.

INSPIRED BY
BURGER KING®
*FRENCH TOAST
STICKS*

INSPIRED BY
EINSTEIN BROS.
BAGELS®
ONION BAGELS

HERBED ONION BAGELS

I created my delightful bagels by combining elements from several recipes.
I enjoy them spread with plain or onion and chive cream cheese.

—Pam Kaiser, Mansfield, MO

PREP: 30 MIN. + CHILLING • **BAKE:** 15 MIN. • **MAKES:** 9 BAGELS

½ cup finely chopped sweet onion
2 Tbsp. butter
¾ cup warm water (70° to 80°)
¼ cup sour cream
3 Tbsp. sugar, divided
3½ tsp. salt, divided
1½ tsp. minced chives
1½ tsp. dried basil
1½ tsp. dried parsley flakes
¾ tsp. dried oregano
¾ tsp. dill weed
¾ tsp. dried minced garlic
3 cups bread flour
1 pkg. (¼ oz.) active dry yeast
3 qt. water
2 Tbsp. yellow cornmeal

WHY YOU'LL LOVE IT...

"These are very tasty bagels with a good chew."
—MARGARETKNOEBEL, TASTEOFHOME.COM

1. In a large skillet, saute onion in butter until tender. In bread machine pan, place the water, sour cream, onion mixture, 2 Tbsp. sugar, 1½ tsp. salt, herbs, garlic, flour and yeast in order suggested by manufacturer. Select dough setting (check dough after 5 minutes of mixing; add 1-2 Tbsp. of water or flour if needed).

2. When cycle is completed, turn dough onto a lightly floured surface. Shape into 9 balls. Push thumb through centers to form a 1½-in. hole. Place on parchment-lined baking sheets. Cover and let rest for 30 minutes, then refrigerate overnight.

3. Let stand at room temperature for 30 minutes; flatten bagels slightly. In a non-aluminum Dutch oven, bring water to a boil with remaining sugar and salt. Drop bagels, 1 at a time, into water. Cook for 30 seconds; turn and cook 30 seconds longer. Remove with a slotted spoon; drain well on paper towels.

4. Sprinkle 2 greased baking sheets with cornmeal; place bagels 2 in. apart on prepared pans. Bake at 425° until golden brown, 12-15 minutes. Remove to wire racks to cool.

1 bagel: 195 cal., 4g fat (2g sat. fat), 11mg chol., 415mg sod., 35g carb. (3g sugars, 2g fiber), 6g pro.

To prepare dough by hand: Dissolve yeast in warm water. In a small bowl, combine sour cream and 2 Tbsp. sugar. In a large bowl, combine, cooked onion mixture, 1½ tsp. salt, herbs, garlic and flour. Add yeast mixture, sour cream mixture and enough water to form a soft dough. Turn onto a floured surface; knead until a smooth, firm dough forms, 8-10 minutes. Cover and let rest 30 minutes in a warm place. Proceed with recipe as written.

HOME FRIES

When I was little, my dad and I would get up early on Sundays and make these for the family.
The rest of the gang would be awakened by the tempting aroma.

—Teresa Koide, Manchester, CT

PREP: 25 MIN. • **COOK:** 15 MIN./BATCH. • **MAKES:** 8 SERVINGS

1 **lb. bacon, chopped**
8 **medium potatoes (about
   3 lbs.), peeled and cut into
   ½-in. pieces**
1 **large onion, chopped**
1 **tsp. salt**
½ **tsp. pepper**

1. In a large skillet, cook chopped bacon over medium-low heat until crisp. Remove bacon from pan with a slotted spoon and drain on paper towels. Remove bacon drippings from pan and reserve.

2. Working in batches, add ¼ cup bacon drippings, potatoes, onion, salt and pepper to pan; toss to coat. Cook and stir over medium-low heat until potatoes are golden brown and tender, 15-20 minutes, adding more drippings as needed. Stir in the cooked bacon; serve immediately.

1 cup: 349 cal., 21g fat (8g sat. fat), 33mg chol., 681mg sod., 31g carb. (3g sugars, 2g fiber), 10g pro.

INSPIRED BY
BOB EVANS®

*GOLDEN BROWN
HOME FRIES*

INSPIRED BY
PEPPERIDGE
FARM®
*BLUEBERRY
TURNOVERS*

BLUEBERRY TURNOVERS

Growing up, I loved to heat up a Pepperidge Farm blueberry turnover for an after-school treat.
I decided I'd try my hand at making them for my kids. I think they are really close, and my kids love them.

—Christine Hair, Tampa, FL

PREP: 45 MIN. • **BAKE:** 15 MIN. • **MAKES:** 8 SERVINGS

---

2 cups fresh or frozen
  blueberries, divided
2 Tbsp. sugar
1 Tbsp. cornstarch
2 tsp. grated lemon zest
2 Tbsp. butter
1 pkg. (17.3 oz.) frozen puff
  pastry, thawed
1 large egg
1 Tbsp. water
½ cup confectioners' sugar
1 Tbsp. 2% milk

1. Preheat oven to 450°. In a large saucepan, combine ½ cup blueberries, sugar, cornstarch and lemon zest. Mash well with a fork. Bring to a boil over low heat; cook and stir until thickened, 1-2 minutes. Remove from heat. Stir in butter and remaining 1½ cups blueberries.

2. Unfold puff pastry. On a lightly floured surface, roll out each pastry sheet into a 12-in. square. Cut each into 4 squares. Spoon 3 Tbsp. filling into the center of each square; fold diagonally in half and press edges to seal. Place on an ungreased baking sheet. Beat egg and water; brush over pastry.

3. Bake until golden brown, 12-15 minutes. Combine confectioners' sugar and milk; drizzle over turnovers. Serve turnovers warm or at room temperature.

Note: If using frozen blueberries, use without thawing to avoid discoloring the batter.

1 turnover: 400 cal., 20g fat (6g sat. fat), 31mg chol., 235mg sod., 51g carb. (14g sugars, 5g fiber), 6g pro.

COPY THAT!

Make sure that you aren't overfilling the blueberry turnovers. While it's tempting to heap on the sweet filling, including more than 3 Tbsp. makes it much more likely that your turnovers will leak. Next, double-check that you're sealing each of the turnovers well enough.

BUTTERMILK PANCAKES

You just can't beat basic buttermilk pancakes for a down-home country breakfast.
These are just like the ones you get at Cracker Barrel. Serve these with sausage and fresh fruit.

—*Betty Abrey, Imperial, SK*

PREP: 10 MIN. • **COOK:** 5 MIN./BATCH • **MAKES:** 2½ DOZEN

4   cups all-purpose flour
¼   cup sugar
2   tsp. baking soda
2   tsp. salt
1½ tsp. baking powder
4   large eggs, room temperature
4   cups buttermilk

1. In a large bowl, combine the flour, sugar, baking soda, salt and baking powder. In another bowl, whisk the eggs and buttermilk until blended; stir into dry ingredients just until moistened.

2. Pour batter by ¼ cupfuls onto a lightly greased hot griddle; turn when bubbles form on top. Cook until second side is golden brown.

Freeze option: Freeze cooled pancakes between layers of waxed paper in a freezer container. To use, place pancakes on an ungreased baking sheet, cover with foil and reheat in a preheated 375° oven 6-10 minutes. Or place a stack of 3 pancakes on a microwave-safe plate and microwave on high until heated through, 45-90 seconds.

3 pancakes: 270 cal., 3g fat (1g sat. fat), 89mg chol., 913mg sod., 48g carb. (11g sugars, 1g fiber), 11g pro.

Pecan Apple Pancakes: To flour mixture, stir in 1¾ tsp. ground cinnamon, ¾ tsp. ground ginger, ¾ tsp. ground mace and ¾ tsp. ground cloves. To batter, fold in 2½ cups shredded peeled apples and ¾ cup chopped pecans.

MOM'S FRIED APPLES

Mom often made these rich cinnamon-sugar apples when I was growing up. I swear the folks at Cracker Barrel copied her recipe!

—*Margie Tappe, Prague, OK*

PREP: 15 MIN. • **COOK:** 30 MIN. • **MAKES:** 8 SERVINGS

½   cup butter, cubed
6   medium unpeeled tart
    red apples, sliced
¾   cup sugar, divided
¾   tsp. ground cinnamon
    Vanilla ice cream, optional

1. Melt butter in a large cast-iron or other ovenproof skillet. Add apples and ½ cup sugar; stir to mix well. Cover and cook over low heat for 20 minutes or until tender, stirring frequently.

2. Add cinnamon and the remaining sugar. Cook and stir over medium-high heat 5-10 minutes longer. If desired, serve with ice cream.

1 serving: 235 cal., 12g fat (7g sat. fat), 31mg chol., 116mg sod., 35g carb. (31g sugars, 3g fiber), 0 pro.

INSPIRED BY CRACKER BARREL®
FRIED APPLES

INSPIRED BY
CRACKER BARREL®
BUTTERMILK
PANCAKES

NEW ORLEANS BEIGNETS

These sweet French doughnuts, inspired by the Cafe Du Monde in New Orleans, are square instead of round and have no hole in the middle. They're a traditional part of breakfast in New Orleans.

—Beth Dawson, Jackson, LA

PREP: 25 MIN. + CHILLING • **COOK:** 5 MIN./BATCH • **MAKES:** 4 DOZEN

1 pkg. (¼ oz.) active dry yeast
¼ cup warm water (110° to 115°)
1 cup evaporated milk
½ cup canola oil
¼ cup sugar
1 large egg, room temperature
4¼ to 4¾ cups self-rising flour
   Oil for deep-fat frying
   Confectioners' sugar

1. In a large bowl, dissolve yeast in warm water. Add milk, oil, sugar, egg and 2 cups flour. Beat until smooth. Stir in enough remaining flour to form a soft dough (dough will be sticky). Do not knead. Cover and refrigerate overnight.

2. Punch down dough. Turn onto a floured surface; roll into a 16x12-in. rectangle. Cut into 2-in. squares.

3. In a deep cast-iron or electric skillet, heat 1 in. oil to 375°. Fry squares, in batches, until golden brown on both sides. Drain on paper towels. Roll warm beignets in confectioners' sugar.

Note: As a substitute for each cup of the self-rising flour, place 1½ tsp. baking powder and ½ tsp. salt in a measuring cup. Add all-purpose flour to measure 1 cup.

1 beignet: 108 cal., 5g fat (1g sat. fat), 6mg chol., 146mg sod., 14g carb. (5g sugars, 0 fiber), 2g pro.

WHY YOU'LL LOVE IT...

"Absolutely fabulous! My daughter wanted beignets for her birthday. I couldn't find the Cafe du Monde mix, so I went with this recipe. They turned out beautifully."
—MARKBRUSICH, TASTEOFHOME.COM

BERRY SMOOTHIE BOWL

I've always loved smoothies but sometimes I want to linger over breakfast instead of sipping it on the go. That's when I make this Jamba-inspired smoothie bowl.

—*Josh Carter, Birmingham, AL*

TAKES: 5 MIN. • **MAKES:** 2 SERVINGS

---

1 cup fat-free milk
1 cup frozen unsweetened strawberries
½ cup frozen unsweetened raspberries
3 Tbsp. sugar
1 cup ice cubes
Optional: Sliced fresh strawberries, fresh raspberries, chia seeds, fresh pumpkin seeds, unsweetened shredded coconut and sliced almonds

Place the milk, berries and sugar in a blender; cover and process until smooth. Add ice cubes; cover and process until smooth. Divide berry mixture between 2 serving bowls. Add toppings as desired.

1½ cups: 155 cal., 0 fat (0 sat. fat), 2mg chol., 54mg sod., 35g carb. (30g sugars, 2g fiber), 5g pro.

HAVE IT YOUR WAY.

Store-bought or homemade granola would add some crunch, while a dollop of peanut butter or honey and a sprinkle of cacao nibs would make your smoothie bowl taste just like dessert. Don't forget a few pieces of your favorite fresh fruit too, such as bananas, blueberries, peaches or even kiwi.

INSPIRED BY JAMBA®
SMOOTHIE BOWL

INSPIRED BY
KRISPY KREME®
ORIGINAL GLAZED
DOUGHNUTS

COPYCAT KRISPY KREME DOUGHNUTS

Glazed warm straight from the fryer, these sweet, heavenly orbs of fried dough
have garnered a loyal cult following that has endured since the first location opened in 1937.

—Lauren Habermehl, Pewaukee, WI

PREP: 15 MIN. + RISING • **COOK:** 5 MIN./BATCH • **MAKES:** 1 DOZEN

1 pkg. (¼ oz.) active dry yeast
¼ cup warm water (110° to 115°)
1 cup warm whole milk
   (110° to 115°)
¼ cup butter, softened
¼ cup sugar
½ tsp. salt
1 large egg, room temperature
3½ to 4 cups all-purpose flour
   Oil for deep-fat frying

GLAZE

2 cups confectioners' sugar
¼ cup whole milk
1 Tbsp. light corn syrup
½ tsp. vanilla extract
⅛ tsp. kosher salt

1. In a large bowl, dissolve yeast in warm water. Add milk, butter, sugar, salt and egg and 2 cups flour. Beat until smooth. Stir in enough flour to form a soft dough.

2. Do not knead. Place in a greased bowl, turning once to grease top. Cover and let rise in a warm place until doubled, about 1 hour.

3. Punch dough down. Turn onto a lightly floured surface; roll out to ½-in. thickness. Cut with a floured 2½-in. doughnut cutter; reroll scraps. Place 1 in. apart on greased baking sheets. Cover and let rise until doubled, 30-45 minutes.

4. In an electric skillet or deep fryer, heat oil to 375°. Fry doughnuts, a few at a time, until golden brown on both sides. Drain on paper towels.

5. For the glaze, whisk together all ingredients; dip warm doughnuts in glaze.

1 doughnut: 339 cal., 15g fat (2g sat. fat), 18mg chol., 98mg sod., 46g carb. (25g sugars, 1g fiber), 4g pro.

POWER BREAKFAST SANDWICH

When I'm looking for a quick breakfast on the go, I always love to have these made and waiting in the freezer.
I can grab one, pop it in the microwave and then head out the door with something nutritious.

—Jolene Martinelli, Fremont, NH

PREP: 20 MIN. • **BAKE:** 15 MIN. • **MAKES:** 6 SERVINGS

1 tsp. olive oil
¼ cup chopped onion
¼ cup chopped sweet red or orange pepper
¼ cup chopped fresh baby spinach
6 large eggs
¼ tsp. salt
¼ tsp. pepper
6 Italian turkey sausage links, casings removed
1 pkg. (12 oz.) multigrain sandwich thins, split
6 slices cheddar, Swiss or pepper jack cheese

1. Preheat oven to 350°. In a large nonstick skillet, heat oil over medium-high heat. Add onion and sweet pepper; cook and stir until tender, 3-4 minutes. Add spinach; cook 1 minute longer. Remove from heat; let cool 5 minutes. In a large bowl, whisk eggs, salt, pepper and onion mixture. Divide egg mixture among 6 greased 4-in. muffin top pan cups. Bake until eggs are set, 12-15 minutes.

2. Meanwhile, shape sausage into six 5-in. patties. In the same skillet, cook patties over medium heat 4-5 minutes on each side or until a thermometer reads 160°. Drain if necessary on paper towels. Layer sandwich bottoms with sausage patties, egg rounds and cheese; replace tops.

Freeze option: Wrap sandwiches in waxed paper and then in foil; freeze in a freezer container. To use, remove foil. Microwave a waxed paper-wrapped sandwich at 50% power until thawed, 1-2 minutes. Turn sandwich over; microwave at 100% power until hot and a thermometer reads at least 165°, 30-60 seconds. Let stand 2 minutes before serving.

1 sandwich: 434 cal., 23g fat (9g sat. fat), 257mg chol., 1026mg sod., 31g carb. (3g sugars, 7g fiber), 30g pro.

INSPIRED BY
DUNKIN®

*POWER BREAKFAST
SANDWICH*

INSPIRED BY
WAFFLE HOUSE®
WAFFLES

LIGHT & FLUFFY WAFFLES

These melt-in-your-mouth waffles are so tender that you can skip butter and syrup, but why would you want to?

—James Schend, Pleasant Prairie, WI

PREP: 15 MIN. + STANDING • **COOK:** 5 MIN./BATCH • **MAKES:** 12 WAFFLES

2 large eggs
1½ cups all-purpose flour
½ cup cornstarch
1 tsp. baking powder
½ tsp. baking soda
½ tsp. salt
½ cup 2% milk
5 Tbsp. canola oil
2 tsp. vanilla extract
1 tsp. white vinegar
2 Tbsp. sugar
½ cup club soda, chilled
Optional: Butter and maple syrup

1. Separate eggs. Place egg whites in a clean, dry bowl; let stand at room temperature 30 minutes.
2. In another bowl, whisk together next 5 ingredients. In a small bowl, whisk egg yolks, milk, oil, vanilla and vinegar until blended. Beat egg whites until soft peaks form. Gradually add sugar; continue beating until stiff peaks form.
3. Preheat waffle maker. Stir together flour mixture, egg yolk mixture and club soda just until combined. Fold egg whites into batter. Bake waffles according to manufacturer's directions until golden brown. Serve with butter and maple syrup if desired.

2 waffles: 312 cal., 14g fat (2g sat. fat), 64mg chol., 421mg sod., 39g carb. (5g sugars, 1g fiber), 6g pro.

PECAN WAFFLES

I've tried for years to duplicate a delicious waffle I sampled at a restaurant here in the South. This crisp and nutty version is what I came up with. Butter and maple syrup are my family's favorite toppings.

—Susan Elise Jansen, Smyrna, GA

TAKES: 30 MIN. • **MAKES:** 10 WAFFLES (4½ IN.)

1¾ cups all-purpose flour
1 Tbsp. baking powder
½ tsp. salt
2 large eggs, separated, room temperature
1¾ cups 2% milk
½ cup canola oil
1 cup chopped pecans
Maple syrup

1. In a bowl, combine flour, baking powder and salt. Combine egg yolks, milk and oil; stir into dry ingredients. Beat egg whites until stiff; fold into batter.
2. Sprinkle hot waffle iron with 2 Tbsp. pecans. Pour ¼-⅓ cup of batter over pecans and bake according to manufacturer's directions until golden brown. Repeat with remaining pecans and batter. Serve with syrup.

2 waffles: 589 cal., 43g fat (5g sat. fat), 83mg chol., 590mg sod., 41g carb. (5g sugars, 3g fiber), 12g pro.

INSPIRED BY WAFFLE HOUSE®
PECAN WAFFLES

CHOCOLATE LOVER'S PANCAKES

These indulgent chocolate pancakes are fluffy on the inside, with a rich but not-too-sweet flavor from the cocoa and a nice tang from the buttermilk. They're delicious with either maple or chocolate syrup—and even better with both swirled together on the plate!

—Harland Johns, Leesburg, TX

PREP: 15 MIN. • **COOK:** 5 MIN./BATCH • **MAKES:** 4 SERVINGS

1 cup all-purpose flour
¼ cup baking cocoa
2 Tbsp. sugar
1 tsp. baking powder
½ tsp. baking soda
½ tsp. salt
1 cup buttermilk
1 large egg, room temperature
2 Tbsp. butter, melted
1 tsp. vanilla extract
  Maple syrup and chocolate syrup

1. In a large bowl, whisk flour, cocoa, sugar, baking powder, baking soda and salt. In another bowl, whisk buttermilk, egg, melted butter and vanilla until blended. Add to the dry ingredients, stirring just until moistened.

2. Place a greased large nonstick skillet over medium heat. In batches, pour batter by ¼ cupfuls onto skillet; cook until bubbles on top begin to pop and bottoms are golden brown. Turn; cook until second side is golden brown. Serve with syrups.

2 pancakes: 271 cal., 8g fat (4g sat. fat), 64mg chol., 753mg sod., 42g carb. (16g sugars, 2g fiber), 8g pro.

INSPIRED BY
IHOP®
*CHOCOLATE
PANCAKES*

INSPIRED BY
PERKINS®

*HAM AND
VEGETABLE
OMELET*

HAM & CHEDDAR OMELET

This cheesy, full-of-flavor omelet is modeled after one I tasted and loved in a local restaurant.
Mine is so hearty and rich tasting that no one will guess it's lower in fat.

—*Bernice Morris, Marshfield, MO*

TAKES: 20 MIN. • **MAKES:** 2 SERVINGS

2   **large eggs**
4   **large egg whites**
¼   **cup fat-free milk**
⅛   **tsp. salt**
⅛   **tsp. pepper**
¼   **cup cubed fully cooked ham**
1   **Tbsp. chopped onion**
1   **Tbsp. chopped green pepper**
¼   **cup shredded reduced-fat cheddar cheese**

1. Whisk together the first 5 ingredients.

2. Place a 10-in. skillet coated with cooking spray over medium heat. Pour in egg mixture. Mixture should set immediately at edges. As eggs set, push cooked portions toward the center, letting uncooked eggs flow underneath. When eggs are thickened and no liquid egg remains, top 1 half with remaining ingredients. Fold omelet in half. Cut in half to serve.

½ omelet: 186 cal., 9g fat (4g sat. fat), 207mg chol., 648mg sod., 4g carb. (3g sugars, 0 fiber), 22g pro. **Diabetic exchanges:** 3 lean meat, 1 fat.

WHY YOU'LL LOVE IT...

"I prepared this omelet for breakfast the other morning and both my husband and I loved it. His one-word review was 'yummo.'"

—MARINEMOM_TEXAS, TASTEOFHOME.COM

CHEWY HONEY GRANOLA BARS

There's sweetness from the honey, chewiness from the raisins, hints of chocolate and cinnamon, and a bit of crunch. To save a few for later, wrap individual bars and place in a resealable freezer container. When you want a satisfying treat on short notice, just grab one and let it thaw for a few minutes.

—Tasha Lehman, Williston, VT

PREP: 10 MIN. • **BAKE:** 15 MIN. + COOLING • **MAKES:** 20 SERVINGS

3 cups old-fashioned oats
2 cups unsweetened puffed
  wheat cereal
1 cup all-purpose flour
⅓ cup chopped walnuts
⅓ cup raisins
⅓ cup miniature semisweet
  chocolate chips
1 tsp. baking soda
1 tsp. ground cinnamon
1 cup honey
¼ cup butter, melted
1 tsp. vanilla extract

1. Preheat oven to 350°. In a large bowl, combine first 8 ingredients. In a small bowl, combine honey, butter and vanilla; pour over oat mixture and mix well. (Mixture will be sticky.)
2. Press into a 13x9-in. baking pan coated with cooking spray. Bake until set and edges are lightly browned, 14-18 minutes. Move to a wire rack to cool completely. Cut into bars.

1 bar: 178 cal., 5g fat (2g sat. fat), 6mg chol., 81mg sod., 32g carb. (17g sugars, 2g fiber), 3g pro. **Diabetic exchanges:** 2 starch, ½ fat.

INSPIRED BY
KIND®

*HONEY OAT
BREAKFAST
BARS*

INSPIRED BY
IHOP®

*STRAWBERRY
& CREAM
CREPES*

CREAMY STRAWBERRY CREPES

Wrap summer-ripe strawberries and creamy filling into these delicate crepes for an elegant brunch entree.

—Kathy Kochiss, Huntington, CT

PREP: 15 MIN. + CHILLING • **COOK:** 35 MIN. • **MAKES:** 7 SERVINGS

4 large eggs, room temperature
1 cup 2% milk
1 cup water
2 Tbsp. butter, melted
2 cups all-purpose flour
¼ tsp. salt

FILLING

1 pkg. (8 oz.) cream cheese, softened
1¼ cups confectioners' sugar
1 Tbsp. lemon juice
1 tsp. grated lemon zest
½ tsp. vanilla extract
4 cups fresh strawberries, sliced, divided
1 cup heavy whipping cream, whipped

COPY THAT!

If you're having a hard time rolling up this dessert crepe recipe, you can fold them instead. Fill and fold in half, fold again and then fold again once more to create a triangular-shaped crepe. You can stack them on top of each other without smearing the filling. (This is a great technique for storing them in the fridge too.)

1. In a large bowl, whisk eggs, milk, water and butter. In another bowl, mix flour and salt; add to egg mixture and mix well. Refrigerate, covered, 1 hour.

2. Heat a lightly greased 8-in. nonstick skillet over medium heat. Stir batter. Fill a ¼-cup measure halfway with batter; pour into center of pan. Quickly lift and tilt pan to coat bottom evenly. Cook until top appears dry; carefully turn crepe over and cook until bottom is cooked, 15-20 seconds longer. Remove to a wire rack. Repeat with remaining batter, greasing pan as needed. When cool, stack crepes between pieces of waxed paper or paper towels.

3. For filling, in a bowl, beat the cream cheese, confectioners' sugar, lemon juice and zest, and vanilla until smooth. Fold in 2 cups berries and the whipped cream. Spoon about ⅓ cup filling down the center of each crepe; roll up. Garnish with remaining berries and, if desired, additional confectioners' sugar. Cover and refrigerate or freeze remaining crepes in an airtight container, unfilled, for another use.

2 crepes: 415 cal., 26g fat (16g sat. fat), 115mg chol., 163mg sod., 40g carb. (28g sugars, 2g fiber), 7g pro.

HOW-TO

Voila, Crepes!

Mastering this French treat is no big deal. Just remember 5 simple words: pour, swirl, flip, fill and serve.

FREEZER BREAKFAST SANDWICHES

On a busy morning, these freezer breakfast sandwiches save the day. A hearty combo of eggs, Canadian bacon and cheese will keep you fueled through lunchtime and beyond.

—Christine Rukavena, Milwaukee, WI

PREP: 25 MIN. • **BAKE:** 15 MIN. • **MAKES:** 12 SANDWICHES

12 large eggs
⅔ cup 2% milk
½ tsp. salt
¼ tsp. pepper

SANDWICHES
12 English muffins, split
4 Tbsp. butter, softened
12 slices Colby-Monterey Jack cheese
12 slices Canadian bacon

1. Preheat oven to 325°. In a large bowl, whisk eggs, milk, salt and pepper until blended. Pour into a 13x9-in. baking pan coated with cooking spray. Bake until set, 15-18 minutes. Cool on a wire rack.

2. Meanwhile, toast English muffins (or bake at 325° until lightly browned, 12-15 minutes). Spread 1 tsp. butter on each muffin bottom.

3. Cut eggs into 12 portions. Layer muffin bottoms with an egg portion, a cheese slice (tearing cheese to fit) and Canadian bacon. Replace muffin tops. Wrap sandwiches in waxed paper and then in foil; freeze in a freezer container.

4. To use frozen sandwiches: Remove foil. Microwave a waxed paper-wrapped sandwich at 50% power until thawed, 1-2 minutes. Turn the sandwich over; microwave at 100% power until hot and a thermometer reads at least 160°, 30-60 seconds. Let stand 2 minutes before serving.

1 sandwich: 334 cal., 17g fat (9g sat. fat), 219mg chol., 759mg sod., 26g carb. (3g sugars, 2g fiber), 19g pro.

INSPIRED BY
MCDONALD'S®
EGG MCMUFFIN

INSPIRED BY
STARBUCKS®
PINK DRINK

COFFEE SHOP FAVORITES

From popular berry beverages and craveworthy coffees to savory snacks and sweet treats, these copycat specialties add a little comfort to your day.

COPYCAT STARBUCKS EGG BITES

These are quick, easy and delicious. I make them ahead for easy breakfasts. You can swap out the Swiss cheese for Gruyere cheese and swap the bacon for ham. I sometime bake these in small Mason jars for a fun presentation. Serve with avocado slices and fresh fruit for a healthy breakfast.

—*Maria Morelli, West Kelowna, BC*

PREP: 10 MIN. • **BAKE:** 25 MIN. • **MAKES:** 6 SERVINGS

6 **large eggs**
¼ **cup 4% cottage cheese**
¼ **tsp. salt**
¼ **tsp. pepper**
½ **cup shredded Swiss cheese**
3 **cooked bacon strips, chopped**

COPY THAT!

Beat the clock in the morning when you prepare these egg bites ahead of time. Simply bake as directed, and store the bites in the freezer. Thaw them overnight in the refrigerator for on-the-go breakfasts.

1. Arrange an oven rack at the lowest rack setting; place a second rack in middle of oven. Place an oven-safe skillet on bottom oven rack; preheat oven and skillet to 300°. Meanwhile, in a small saucepan, bring 2 cups water to a boil.
2. In a blender, puree the first 4 ingredients until smooth, about 20 seconds. Line 6 muffin cups with foil liners. Divide Swiss cheese and bacon among the muffin cups. Pour egg mixture over top.
3. Wearing oven mitts, place muffin tin on top rack. Pull bottom rack out 6-8 in.; add boiling water to skillet. (Work quickly and carefully, pouring water away from you. Don't worry if some water is left in the saucepan.) Carefully slide bottom rack back into place; quickly close door to trap steam in oven.
4. Bake until the eggs puff and are cooked to desired degree of doneness, 25-30 minutes. Serve immediately.
1 egg bite: 143 cal., 10g fat (4g sat. fat), 201mg chol., 311mg sod., 1g carb. (1g sugars, 0 fiber), 12g pro.

INSPIRED BY
STARBUCKS®
EGG BITES

INSPIRED BY STARBUCKS®

PUMPKIN BREAD

COPYCAT STARBUCKS PUMPKIN BREAD

Skip the line! Make Starbucks pumpkin bread in your own kitchen and let the aroma fill your home as it bakes. This copycat recipe is a definite keeper!

—Taste of Home *Test Kitchen*

PREP: 25 MIN. • **BAKE:** 1 HOUR + COOLING • **MAKES:** 2 LOAVES (16 SLICES EACH)

1 can (15 oz.) solid-pack pumpkin
4 large eggs
¾ cup canola oil
⅔ cup water
2 cups sugar
1 cup honey
1½ tsp. vanilla extract
3½ cups all-purpose flour
2 tsp. baking soda
1½ tsp. salt
1½ tsp. ground cinnamon
1 tsp. ground nutmeg
½ tsp. ground cloves
½ tsp. ground ginger
½ cup salted pumpkin seeds
  or pepitas

1. Preheat oven to 350°. In a large bowl, beat pumpkin, eggs, oil, water, sugar, honey and vanilla until well blended. In another bowl, whisk flour, baking soda, salt and spices; gradually beat into pumpkin mixture.

2. Transfer to 2 greased 9x5-in. loaf pans. Sprinkle tops with pumpkin seeds.

3. Bake 60-70 minutes or until a toothpick inserted in center comes out clean. Cool in pan 10 minutes before removing to a wire rack to cool.

1 slice: 202 cal., 7g fat (1g sat. fat), 23mg chol., 205mg sod., 33g carb. (22g sugars, 1g fiber), 3g pro.

HAVE IT YOUR WAY.

Numerous mix-ins work well with pumpkin bread. We recommend adding chocolate chips or nuts and fruit.

COLD-BREW COFFEE

Cold brewing reduces the acidity of coffee, which enhances its natural sweetness and complex flavors. Even those who take hot coffee with sugar and cream might find themselves sipping cold brew plain.
—Taste of Home *Test Kitchen*

PREP: 10 MIN. + CHILLING • **MAKES:** 8 SERVINGS

1 cup coarsely ground medium-roast coffee
1 cup hot water (205°)
6 to 7 cups cold water
Optional: 2% milk or half-and-half cream

1. Place the coffee grounds in a clean glass container. Pour hot water over the grounds; let stand 10 minutes. Stir in cold water. Cover and refrigerate mixture 12-24 hours. (The longer it sits, the stronger the flavor.)
2. Strain coffee through a fine-mesh sieve; discard grounds. Strain coffee again through a coffee filter; discard grounds. Serve over ice, with milk or cream if desired. Store in refrigerator for up to 2 weeks.
1 cup: 2 cal., 0 fat (0 sat. fat), 0 chol., 4mg sod., 0 carb. (0 sugars, 0 fiber), 0 pro.

DID YOU KNOW?

Some people enjoy a tiny pinch of salt instead of sugar in cold brews. Salt actually brings out the inherent sweetness of the coffee.

MOCHA MORNING DRINK

When I'm sipping this delicious coffee, I almost feel as if I'm visiting my favorite coffeehouse.
—*Jill Rodriguez, Gonzales, LA*

TAKES: 15 MIN. • **MAKES:** 6 SERVINGS

6 cups hot brewed coffee
¾ cup half-and-half cream
6 Tbsp. chocolate syrup
7 tsp. sugar
6 cinnamon sticks (3 in.)
Whipped cream in a can, optional

In a large saucepan, combine the coffee, cream, chocolate syrup and sugar. Cook and stir over medium heat until the sugar is dissolved and mixture is heated through. Ladle into 6 large mugs. Stir each serving with a cinnamon stick. Garnish with whipped cream if desired.
1 cup: 116 cal., 3g fat (2g sat. fat), 15mg chol., 29mg sod., 19g carb. (16g sugars, 1g fiber), 2g pro.
Diabetic exchanges: ½ starch, ½ milk.

INSPIRED BY STARBUCKS®
CAFFE MOCHA

INSPIRED BY
STARBUCKS®
ICED COFFEE

INSPIRED BY
STARBUCKS®

*CRANBERRY
BLISS BARS*

HEAVENLY ORANGE CRANBERRY BARS

You can bake Starbucks cranberry bliss bars any time you please with this copycat recipe.
It makes an entire pan of bars that taste just like the real deal.

—Jennifer Blakely, Visalia, CA

PREP: 30 MIN. + CHILLING • **BAKE:** 20 MIN. + COOLING • **MAKES:** 8 DOZEN

1½ cups packed brown sugar
1 cup butter, melted
2 large eggs, room temperature
2 tsp. vanilla extract
2¼ cups all-purpose flour
1 tsp. baking powder
1 tsp. salt
1 cup white baking chips
1 cup dried cranberries, coarsely chopped
1 cup chopped pecans, toasted
¼ cup grated orange zest

FROSTING

1 pkg. (8 oz.) cream cheese, softened
1 cup confectioners' sugar
½ cup butter, softened
3 Tbsp. grated orange zest, divided
2 tsp. vanilla extract
⅓ cup dried cranberries, coarsely chopped

1. Preheat oven to 350°. In a large bowl, beat brown sugar, melted butter, eggs and vanilla until well blended. In another bowl, whisk flour, baking powder and salt; gradually beat into sugar mixture. Stir in baking chips, cranberries, pecans and orange zest.

2. Spread into a greased 15x10x1-in. baking pan. Bake until a toothpick inserted in the center comes out clean, 18-22 minutes. Cool completely in pan on a wire rack.

3. For frosting, in a large bowl, combine cream cheese, confectioners' sugar, butter, 1 Tbsp. zest and vanilla; beat until smooth. Spread over the bars. Combine dried cranberries and remaining 2 Tbsp. zest; sprinkle over frosting. Refrigerate at least 2 hours. Cut into triangles. Store in the refrigerator.

1 triangle: 89 cal., 5g fat (3g sat. fat), 14mg chol., 64mg sod., 10g carb. (7g sugars, 0 fiber), 1g pro.

WHY YOU'LL LOVE IT...

"I first made these bars for Thanksgiving, and they came out great. My brother-in-law renamed them A Little Taste of Christmas, and that has stuck. Just made them again last night!"
—SANDY202, TASTEOFHOME.COM

PINK DRINK

Whether you've seen it at the beach or on your favorite Instagram account, the Starbucks Pink Drink is still one of the most beautiful beverages we know. Now you can create your own version of the strawberry refresher.

—Taste of Home *Test Kitchen*

PREP: 15 MIN. + CHILLING. • **COOK:** 20 MIN. • **MAKES:** 2 SERVINGS

1 cup frozen unsweetened strawberries, thawed
2 berry-flavored green tea bags
1 cup boiling water
1½ cups coconut milk, chilled
2 Tbsp. simple syrup
2 cups ice cubes
¼ cup freeze-dried strawberries, slightly crushed

1. In a saucepan, cook strawberries over low heat until they start to break apart, about 15 minutes, stirring occasionally. Remove from heat; cool. Using an immersion blender, puree strawberries. Chill, covered, until ready to serve.

2. Steep tea 5 minutes in boiling water; discard tea bags. Stir in strawberry mixture, coconut milk and simple syrup. Divide mixture between 2 glasses filled with ice. Garnish with strawberries.

1½ cups: 367 cal., 27g fat (27g sat. fat), 0 chol., 47mg sod., 28g carb. (23g sugars, 3g fiber), 4g pro.

INSPIRED BY
STARBUCKS®
PINK DRINK

INSPIRED BY
STARBUCKS®
CAKE POPS

FUN & FESTIVE CAKE POPS

When looking for a little nibble at a coffee shop, lots of people go for a cake pop. With this recipe, you can make your own, even changing flavors to match the occasion or season of the year.
—Taste of Home *Test Kitchen*

PREP: 1 HOUR • **BAKE:** 35 MIN. + FREEZING • **MAKES:** 4 DOZEN

1 pkg. cake mix of your choice (regular size)
1 cup prepared frosting of your choice
48 lollipop sticks
2½ lbs. dark chocolate, milk chocolate or white candy coating, coarsely chopped
Optional toppings: Crushed peppermint candies, finely chopped cashews, unsweetened coconut, assorted sprinkles, finely chopped crystallized ginger, crushed gingersnap cookies, melted caramels and coarse sea salt

1. Prepare and bake cake mix according to package directions, using a greased 13x9-in. baking pan. Cool completely on a wire rack.

2. Crumble cake into a large bowl. Add frosting and mix well. Shape into 1½-in. balls. Place on baking sheets; insert sticks. Freeze for at least 2 hours or refrigerate for at least 3 hours or until cake balls are firm.

3. In a microwave, melt candy coating. Dip each cake ball into coating; allow excess to drip off. Roll, sprinkle or drizzle with toppings of your choice. Insert cake pops into a foam block to stand. Let stand until set.

1 cake pop: 213 cal., 11g fat (7g sat. fat), 13mg chol., 97mg sod., 28g carb. (23g sugars, 1g fiber), 1g pro.

COPY THAT!

If you are new to making cake pops, keep decorating simple and organized from the get-go. Start by making sure to freeze or chill the cake balls before dipping and decorating. Rather than dealing with melted chocolate, use confectioners' candy coatings, wafers, candy melts or other coatings specifically designed for cake pops. Keep various sprinkles and toppings in their own dishes and have them ready to go before you begin.

PUMPKIN LATTE

Don't wait for your favorite coffee shop to bring back pumpkin lattes—make your own all year with this recipe. With just the right amount of spice, it tastes like the popular version everyone adores.

—Taste of Home *Test Kitchen*

TAKES: 15 MIN. • **MAKES:** 2 SERVINGS

2 cups whole milk
2 Tbsp. canned pumpkin
2 Tbsp. sugar
2 Tbsp. vanilla extract
½ tsp. pumpkin pie spice
½ cup hot brewed espresso
Optional: Whipped cream, pumpkin pie spice and ground nutmeg

1. In a small saucepan, combine milk, pumpkin and sugar. Cook and stir over medium heat until steaming. Remove from heat; stir in vanilla and the pie spice. Transfer to a blender; cover and process for 15 seconds or until foamy.
2. Pour into 2 mugs; add espresso. Garnish with whipped cream and spices if desired.
1¼ cups: 234 cal., 8g fat (5g sat. fat), 33mg chol., 122mg sod., 26g carb. (24g sugars, 1g fiber), 8g pro.

CARAMEL FRAPPUCCINO

I love Frappuccinos from Starbucks, but they get too expensive. I now make my own that are just as good. If you blend the milk with all the other ingredients, it gets too foamy—instead stir it in with a spoon after all the ice is crushed.

—Heather Egger, Davenport, IA

PREP: 10 MIN. + CHILLING • **MAKES:** 4 CUPS

2 Tbsp. ground dark coffee
1 cup water
3 Tbsp. sugar
2 Tbsp. caramel ice cream topping
2 cups ice cubes
1 cup fat-free milk
Whipped cream, optional

1. Place ground coffee in the coffee filter of a drip coffeemaker. Add water; brew according to manufacturer's directions. Refrigerate coffee until cold.
2. In a blender, combine cold coffee, sugar, caramel topping and ice cubes; process until smooth. Add milk and pulse to combine. Pour into glasses. If desired, top with whipped cream and additional caramel topping.
2 cups: 159 cal., 0 fat (0 sat. fat), 2mg chol., 122mg sod., 37g carb. (37g sugars, 0 fiber), 4g pro.

INSPIRED BY STARBUCKS®
CARAMEL FRAPPUCCINO

INSPIRED BY
STARBUCKS®

*PUMPKIN
SPICE LATTE*

INSPIRED BY
DOLLYWOOD®

*CINNAMON
BREAD*

COPYCAT DOLLYWOOD CINNAMON BREAD

Whenever I go to Dollywood, the first thing I do is run to the Grist Mill to get in line for the cinnamon bread. It's that good! I tried making it at home and think I got pretty close. I like using pumpkin pie spice instead of just cinnamon to give it a little more flavor.
—*Amanda Singleton, Kingsport, TN*

PREP: 30 MIN. + RISING • **BAKE:** 30 MIN. + COOLING • **MAKES:** 1 LOAF (16 PIECES)

1 pkg. (¼ oz.) active dry yeast
1¼ cups warm 2% milk
    (110° to 115°)
2½ cups bread flour
⅓ cup butter, melted
2 Tbsp. sugar
1 large egg, room temperature
¾ tsp. salt
2 to 2½ cups all-purpose flour

TOPPING

¼ cup sugar
2 tsp. pumpkin pie spice, apple pie spice or ground cinnamon
¼ cup butter, melted

1. In a large bowl, dissolve yeast in warm milk. Add bread flour, butter, sugar, egg and salt. Beat on medium speed for 3 minutes. Stir in enough all-purpose flour to form a firm dough.

2. Turn onto a floured surface; knead until smooth and elastic, 6-8 minutes. Place in a greased bowl, turning once to grease the top. Cover and let rise in a warm place until doubled, about 1 hour.

3. In a pie plate, combine sugar and pie spice. Pour melted butter into another pie plate. Punch dough down. Turn onto a lightly floured surface. Shape into a loaf. Using a sharp knife, make 4 very deep slits straight across bread dough (without cutting all the way through the loaf). Roll dough in butter, massaging butter onto all surfaces until the dough is thoroughly coated. Roll dough in sugar mixture, firmly pressing mixture onto dough. Place dough in a parchment-lined 9x5-in. loaf pan. Cover and let rise in a warm place until doubled, 30 minutes. Meanwhile, preheat oven to 350°.

4. Bake until golden brown, 30-40 minutes. (Cover loosely with foil if top browns too quickly.) Cool 10 minutes before removing from pan to a wire rack. Serve warm.

1 piece: 215 cal., 7g fat (4g sat. fat), 27mg chol., 167mg sod., 34g carb. (6g sugars, 1g fiber), 5g pro.

Speedy Cinnamon Bread: If you don't feel like making your own dough, you can use a thawed 1-lb. frozen bread loaf.

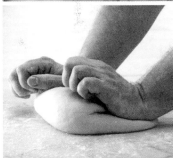

YOGURT BERRY PARFAITS

Inspired by the Berry Trio Parfait at my local Starbucks, I layered homemade granola with fresh fruit and yogurt. It makes a superb breakfast.
—*Donna Speirs, Kennebunk, ME*

PREP: 30 MIN. • **BAKE:** 35 MIN. + COOLING • **MAKES:** 8 SERVINGS

2 cups old-fashioned oats
½ cup pecan halves
½ cup sliced almonds
¼ cup sunflower kernels
½ cup packed brown sugar
½ tsp. salt
¼ cup butter, cubed
¼ cup honey
½ tsp. ground cinnamon
1 tsp. vanilla extract
½ cup dried cherries
½ cup dried blueberries

PARFAITS
2 cups fresh blueberries
2 cups fresh raspberries
2 cups chopped fresh strawberries
4 cups honey Greek yogurt

1. Preheat the oven to 350°. In a large bowl, combine the first 6 ingredients. In a small saucepan, mix butter, honey and cinnamon. Cook over medium heat until blended, 3-4 minutes. Remove from heat; stir in vanilla. Pour over oat mixture; stir to coat.

2. Spread evenly into a greased 15x10x1-in. baking pan. Bake until crisp and dark golden brown, 35-40 minutes, stirring every 10 minutes. Cool completely on a wire rack. Stir in dried fruit.

3. In a small bowl, combine berries. Layer ¼ cup each berries, yogurt and granola in 8 parfait glasses. Repeat layers. Top with the remaining berries.

1 parfait: 590 cal., 27g fat (11g sat. fat), 42mg chol., 294mg sod., 81g carb. (55g sugars, 9g fiber), 10g pro.

INSPIRED BY
STARBUCKS®

BERRY TRIO
PARFAIT

INSPIRED BY
KFC®

CHILI LIME
FRIED CHICKEN

BEST
APPETIZERS
EVER

Turn here the next time you are entertaining, need a dish to pass or simply want a savory late-night bite.

CAJUN FRIES WITH MALT VINEGAR SAUCE

Five Guys' fries have tons of devotees—and for good reason. My family is partial to the Cajun fries, specifically, which are super easy to make at home with your own seasoning blend. Air-fried instead of deep-fried, this salty, smoky, subtly sweet recipe is better for you than the original but is just as tasty!

—*Julie Peterson, Crofton, MD*

TAKES: 30 MIN. • **MAKES:** 4 SERVINGS

1 lb. russet potatoes
1½ tsp. peanut oil

CAJUN SEASONING
1 tsp. sugar
1 tsp. smoked paprika
½ tsp. salt
½ tsp. garlic powder
½ tsp. onion powder
½ tsp. crushed red pepper flakes
½ tsp. dried oregano

DIPPING SAUCE
¼ cup mayonnaise
¼ cup ketchup
4½ tsp. malt vinegar

Preheat air fryer to 400°. Cut potatoes into ¼-in. julienned strips; toss with oil. Combine Cajun seasoning ingredients. Sprinkle over potatoes; toss to coat. Place potatoes in greased air fryer. Cook until browned and crisp, 12-14 minutes, shaking once to redistribute. Combine dipping sauce ingredients; serve with fries.

Note: In our testing, we find that cook times vary dramatically between brands of air fryers. As a result, we give wider than normal ranges on suggested cook times. Begin checking at the first time listed and adjust as needed.

1 serving: 216 cal., 12g fat (2g sat. fat), 5mg chol., 563mg sod., 26g carb. (6g sugars, 3g fiber), 3g pro.

Oven Version: Prepare potatoes as directed. Place on a greased baking sheet. Bake at 450° until golden brown and crispy, 18-20 minutes, turning once. Serve with sauce.

INSPIRED BY
FIVE GUYS®
CAJUN FRIES

**INSPIRED BY
CHIPOTLE®**

QUESO BLANCO

WHITE CHEESE DIP

My family loves the Queso Blanco from Chipotle, so I made it my mission to re-create it at home.
After many failed attempts, did I succeed? You be the judge! We think the result is amazing.
—*Amy Enoch, Carthage, TN*

TAKES: 20 MIN. • **MAKES:** 3 CUPS

20 slices white American cheese, chopped (such as Kraft singles)
1 cup heavy whipping cream
6 Tbsp. salsa verde
3 Tbsp. juice from pickled jalapeno slices
3 Tbsp. pickled jalapeno slices, finely chopped
1½ tsp. reduced-sodium taco seasoning
Tortilla chips

Combine all ingredients in a large microwave-safe bowl. Microwave, covered, on high until mixture is smooth and heated through, about 6-7 minutes, stirring frequently. Serve warm with tortilla chips.

¼ cup : 139 cal., 14g fat (9g sat. fat), 45mg chol., 68mg sod., 2g carb. (1g sugars, 0 fiber), 1g pro.

HOMEMADE GUACAMOLE

I always judge a Tex-Mex restaurant by its guacamole: Although it's simple to prepare, it can go wrong oh so easily. I've spent many years perfecting mine to the point where I think it's better than in most restaurants.
—*Joan Hallford, North Richland Hills, TX*

TAKES: 10 MIN. • **MAKES:** 2 CUPS

3 medium ripe avocados, peeled and cubed
1 garlic clove, minced
¼ to ½ tsp. salt
1 small onion, finely chopped
1 to 2 Tbsp. lime juice
1 Tbsp. minced fresh cilantro
2 medium tomatoes, seeded and chopped, optional
¼ cup mayonnaise, optional

Mash avocados with garlic and salt. Stir in the remaining ingredients, adding tomatoes and mayonnaise if desired.

¼ cup: 90 cal., 8g fat (1g sat. fat), 0 chol., 78mg sod., 6g carb. (1g sugars, 4g fiber), 1g pro.
Diabetic exchanges: 1½ fat.

INSPIRED BY CHIPOTLE®
GUACAMOLE AND CHIPS

MINI MAC & CHEESE BITES

Young relatives were coming for a party, so I wanted something fun for them to eat.
To my surprise, it was the adults who devoured these mini mac and cheese bites.
—*Kate Mainiero, Elizaville, NY*

PREP: 35 MIN. • **BAKE:** 10 MIN. • **MAKES:** 3 DOZEN

2 cups uncooked elbow macaroni
1 cup seasoned bread crumbs, divided
2 Tbsp. butter
2 Tbsp. all-purpose flour
½ tsp. onion powder
½ tsp. garlic powder
½ tsp. seasoned salt
1¾ cups 2% milk
2 cups shredded sharp cheddar cheese, divided
1 cup shredded Swiss cheese
¾ cup biscuit/baking mix
2 large eggs, room temperature, lightly beaten

1. Preheat oven to 425°. Cook macaroni according to package directions; drain.
2. Meanwhile, sprinkle ¼ cup bread crumbs into 36 greased mini-muffin cups. In a large saucepan, melt butter over medium heat. Stir in flour and the seasonings until smooth; gradually whisk in milk. Bring to a boil, stirring constantly; cook and stir until thickened, 1-2 minutes. Stir in 1 cup cheddar cheese and the Swiss cheese until melted.
3. Remove from heat; stir in biscuit mix, eggs and ½ cup bread crumbs. Add macaroni; toss to coat. Spoon about 2 Tbsp. macaroni mixture into prepared mini-muffin cups; sprinkle with remaining cheddar cheese and bread crumbs.
4. Bake until golden brown, 8-10 minutes. Cool in pans for 5 minutes before serving.

1 appetizer: 91 cal., 5g fat (3g sat. fat), 22mg chol., 162mg sod., 8g carb. (1g sugars, 0 fiber), 4g pro.

HAVE IT YOUR WAY.

Customize these bites by adding mix-ins like chopped jalapenos, cooked and crumbled bacon, diced green onion, chopped parsley, or minced garlic.

INSPIRED BY
NOODLES &
COMPANY®
POT STICKERS

PORK & CHIVE POT STICKERS

Here's my top make-ahead appetizer. They have the same flavor you'd find in a restaurant but are a bit lighter. My three kids are old enough to reheat these right from the freezer.
—*Marisa Raponi, Vaughan, ON*

PREP: 1 HOUR • **COOK:** 5 MIN./BATCH • **MAKES:** 5 DOZEN

2 medium carrots, finely chopped
1 small onion, finely chopped
½ cup finely chopped water chestnuts
⅓ cup minced fresh chives
1 large egg white, lightly beaten
3 Tbsp. reduced-sodium soy sauce
½ tsp. pepper
1 lb. ground pork
60 pot sticker or gyoza wrappers
3 Tbsp. canola oil, divided
1 cup chicken broth, divided

WHY YOU'LL LOVE IT...

"My husband loves these from a Chinese restaurant, so I am thrilled to have a copycat recipe to make my own. These are so good!"
—PATTIEJEAN, TASTEOFHOME.COM

1. In a large bowl, combine the first 7 ingredients. Add pork; mix lightly but thoroughly. Place 1 scant Tbsp. filling in center of each wrapper. (Cover remaining wrappers with a damp paper towel until ready to use.)
2. Moisten wrapper edges with water. Fold wrapper over filling; seal edges, pleating the front side several times to form a pleated pouch. Stand pot stickers on a work surface to flatten bottoms; curve slightly to form crescent shapes if desired.
3. In a large nonstick skillet, heat 1 Tbsp. oil over medium-high heat. Arrange a third of the pot stickers in concentric circles in pan, flat side down; cook until bottoms are golden brown, 1-2 minutes.
4. Carefully add ⅓ cup broth (broth may splatter); reduce heat to medium-low. Cook, covered, until broth is almost absorbed and filling is cooked through, 2-3 minutes. Uncover; cook until bottoms are crisp and broth is completely evaporated, about 1 minute. Repeat with remaining oil, pot stickers and broth. If desired, serve with additional soy sauce and top with additional chives.

Freeze option: Place uncooked pot stickers on waxed paper-lined baking sheets; freeze until firm. Transfer to airtight freezer containers; return to freezer. To use, cook frozen pot stickers as directed, increasing broth to ½ cup and simmering time to 4-6 minutes for each batch.

Note: Wonton wrappers may be substituted for pot sticker and gyoza wrappers. Stack 2 or 3 wonton wrappers on a work surface; cut into circles with a 3½-in. biscuit or round cookie cutter. Fill and wrap as directed.

1 pot sticker: 39 cal., 2g fat (0 sat. fat), 6mg chol., 66mg sod., 4g carb. (0 sugars, 0 fiber), 2g pro.

SPICY CHICKEN WINGS WITH BLUE CHEESE DIP

These fall-off-the-bone tender wings have just the right amount of heat,
and cool blue cheese dressing creates the perfect flavor combination for dipping.
—*Kevalyn Henderson, Hayward, WI*

PREP: 25 MIN. + MARINATING • **BAKE:** 2 HOURS • **MAKES:** 2 DOZEN (1¾ CUPS DIP)

1   cup reduced-sodium soy sauce
⅔   cup sugar
2   tsp. salt
2   tsp. grated orange zest
2   garlic cloves, minced
½   tsp. pepper
3   lbs. chicken wingettes and
    drumettes
3   tsp. chili powder
¾   tsp. cayenne pepper
¾   tsp. hot pepper sauce

BLUE CHEESE DIP

1   cup mayonnaise
½   cup blue cheese
    salad dressing
⅓   cup buttermilk
2   tsp. Italian salad dressing mix

1. In a small bowl, combine soy sauce, sugar, salt, orange zest, garlic and pepper. Pour half the marinade into a large shallow dish. Add chicken; turn to coat. Cover and refrigerate for 1 hour. Cover and refrigerate remaining marinade.

2. Drain the chicken, discarding marinade. Transfer chicken to a greased 13x9-in. baking dish. Cover and bake at 325° for 1½ hours or until chicken juices run clear.

3. Using tongs, transfer chicken to a greased 15x10x1-in. baking pan. In a small bowl, combine the chili powder, cayenne, pepper sauce and reserved marinade. Drizzle over chicken.

4. Bake, uncovered, for 30 minutes, turning once. In a small bowl, whisk the dip ingredients. Serve with wings.

1 serving: 237 cal., 19g fat (4g sat. fat), 47mg chol., 588mg sod., 4g carb. (3g sugars, 0 fiber), 11g pro.

INSPIRED BY
OUTBACK
STEAKHOUSE®
*SPICY
KOOKABURRA WINGS*

INSPIRED BY
HOULIHAN'S®

*HOULIHAN'S
SHROOMS*

COPYCAT HOULIHAN'S SHROOMS

I enjoyed this appetizer at Houlihan's restaurant and ordered it every time I went there. When the restaurant closed in my area, I was determined to re-create the dish at home. The mushrooms might even be better than the restaurant's. Besides baking them, I have also cooked them on a grill and in a toaster oven. Consistently delicious, the stuffed mushrooms are enjoyed every single time.

—Jo Hart, Flippin, AR

PREP: 25 MIN. • **BAKE:** 15 MIN. • **MAKES:** ABOUT 1½ DOZEN

1 **lb. small fresh portobello mushrooms**
4 **Tbsp. butter, divided**
⅓ **cup finely chopped onion**
1 **pkg. (8 oz.) cream cheese, cubed**
½ **tsp. seasoned salt**
⅓ **cup finely shredded cheddar cheese**

TOPPING
¼ **cup crushed Ritz crackers**
1 **Tbsp. butter, melted**

1. Preheat oven to 375°. Remove stems from mushrooms and finely chop stems; set caps aside. In a large skillet, melt 2 Tbsp. butter over medium heat. Add chopped stems and onion; cook and stir until tender, 4-6 minutes.

2. Add cream cheese and seasoned salt; cook and stir until cream cheese is melted. Fill mushroom caps. Melt remaining 2 Tbsp. butter. Dip bottoms of mushrooms in melted butter; place on a baking sheet. Top with cheddar cheese. For topping, combine crackers and butter; sprinkle over tops.

3. Bake 12-15 minutes or until the mushrooms are tender and heated through. Serve hot.

1 stuffed mushroom: 95 cal., 9g fat (5g sat. fat), 23mg chol., 131mg sod., 3g carb. (1g sugars, 0 fiber), 2g pro.

COPYCAT CHEESECAKE FACTORY CHEESEBURGER EGG ROLLS

Filled with juicy ground beef, a smattering of crumbled bacon, diced pickles and plenty of melty cheddar cheese, these crunchy wonton-wrapped wonders are a Cheesecake Factory bestseller for a reason. Now you can whip up a batch at home.

—Taste of Home *Test Kitchen*

PREP: 30 MIN. • **COOK:** 20 MIN. • **MAKES:** 1 DOZEN (1½ CUPS SAUCE)

1 lb. ground beef
1 small onion, chopped
2 garlic cloves, minced
1 cup shredded cheddar cheese
½ cup chopped dill pickles
4 bacon strips, cooked and crumbled
1 Tbsp. Worcestershire sauce
1 Tbsp. yellow mustard
1 Tbsp. ketchup
¼ tsp. salt
¼ tsp. pepper
14 egg roll wrappers
1 large egg, lightly beaten
  Oil for deep-fat frying

DIPPING SAUCE
1 cup mayonnaise
½ cup ketchup
½ tsp. garlic powder
½ tsp. paprika

HAVE IT YOUR WAY.

For gluten-free cheeseburger egg rolls, swap in spring roll wrappers for the traditional wonton wrappers. Spring roll wrappers are made with rice flour rather than wheat flour, so they're typically safe for those who need to avoid gluten. If you are especially sensitive, we recommend checking the label to ensure the wrappers have been processed in a facility that is gluten-free certified.

1. In a large skillet, cook beef, onion and garlic over medium heat until beef is no longer pink and onion is tender, 4-5 minutes, breaking up beef into crumbles; drain. Return to pan. Stir in the cheese, pickles, crumbled bacon, Worcestershire sauce, mustard, ketchup, salt and pepper.
2. With 1 corner of an egg roll wrapper facing you, place about ⅓ cup filling just below center of wrapper. (Cover remaining wrappers with a damp paper towel until ready to use.) Fold bottom corner over filling; moisten remaining wrapper edges with beaten egg. Fold side corners toward center over filling. Roll egg roll up tightly, pressing at tip to seal. Repeat.
3. In an electric skillet or deep-fat fryer, heat oil to 375°. Fry egg rolls, a few at a time, until golden brown, 3-4 minutes, turning occasionally. Drain on paper towels.
4. Combine sauce ingredients; serve with egg rolls.

1 egg roll with 2 Tbsp. sauce: 451 cal., 32g fat (7g sat. fat), 61mg chol., 712mg sod., 26g carb. (4g sugars, 1g fiber), 14g pro.

EASY EGG ROLLS

Preparing egg rolls is a snap with these tips:
• Drain the fat well from the cooked beef to make the egg rolls crunchy.
• For successful folding and rolling, be sure not to overstuff the egg rolls with filling.
• It's important to turn the egg rolls while frying so they brown on all sides.

INSPIRED BY
CHEESECAKE FACTORY®
CHEESEBURGER EGG ROLLS

INSPIRED BY
CALIFORNIA
PIZZA
KITCHEN®

*HOT
SPINACH
DIP*

SPICY SPINACH & ARTICHOKE DIP

This is my take on California Pizza Kitchen's Hot Spinach Dip. I added artichoke hearts for extra tastiness and texture plus chiles for a kick. I always use a flavored salt, such as celery salt, for more flavor.
—Michaela Rosenthal, Woodland Hills, CA

PREP: 20 MIN. • **BAKE:** 40 MIN. • **MAKES:** 3 CUPS

1 pkg. (8 oz.) cream cheese, softened
⅓ cup mayonnaise
¼ cup shredded Parmesan cheese
¼ cup shredded Asiago cheese
1 tsp. dried minced garlic
1 tsp. dried parsley flakes
½ tsp. celery salt
1 can (14 oz.) water-packed artichoke hearts, drained and coarsely chopped
5 oz. frozen chopped spinach, thawed and squeezed dry (about ½ cup)
1 can (4 oz.) chopped green chiles, drained
1 jar (2 oz.) diced pimientos, drained
⅓ cup shredded part-skim mozzarella cheese
  Tortilla chips or cubed sourdough bread

1. Preheat the oven to 350°. In a large bowl, beat the first 7 ingredients until combined. Stir in artichokes, spinach, chiles and pimientos. Transfer to a greased 3-cup baking dish; sprinkle with mozzarella. Place on a rimmed baking sheet.
2. Bake until hot and bubbly, 40-45 minutes. Serve with tortilla chips or bread.

¼ cup: 150 cal., 13g fat (6g sat. fat), 27mg chol., 324mg sod., 5g carb. (1g sugars, 1g fiber), 5g pro.

WHY YOU'LL LOVE IT...

"This was delicious! I love Asiago cheese, and it goes so nicely in this dish. It's an easy crowd-pleaser!"
—XXCSKIER, TASTEOFHOME.COM

CRISPY CRAB RANGOON

My husband loved the appetizers we had at P.F. Chang's so much, I was determined to make them at home. After several more trips to that restaurant to taste them again, I had them perfected. I often prepare the filling earlier in the day to save time later.

—*Cathy Blankman, Warroad, MN*

TAKES: 30 MIN. • **MAKES:** 16 APPETIZERS

- 3 oz. cream cheese, softened
- 2 green onions, finely chopped
- ¼ cup finely chopped imitation crabmeat
- 1 tsp. minced garlic
- 16 wonton wrappers
  Oil for frying
  Sweet-and-sour sauce

1. In a small bowl, beat cream cheese until smooth. Stir in onions, crab and garlic.

2. Place about 1½ tsp. in the center of a wonton wrapper. (Keep remaining wrappers covered with a damp paper towel until ready to use.) Moisten edges with water; fold opposite corners over filling and press to seal. Repeat.

3. In an electric skillet, heat 1 in. oil to 375°. Fry wontons, in batches, until golden brown, about 1 minute on each side. Drain on paper towels. Serve with sweet-and-sour sauce.

1 rangoon: 61 cal., 4g fat (1g sat. fat), 6mg chol., 77mg sod., 5g carb. (0 sugars, 0 fiber), 1g pro.

COPY THAT!

If you want to assemble these appetizers ahead of time, freeze the uncooked crab rangoons in an airtight container for at least 1 hour or until solid. Fry them immediately after removing from the freezer.

SPICY EDAMAME

Edamame are young soybeans in their pods. People love ordering them alongside sushi, but now you can whip them up at home.

—Taste of Home *Test Kitchen*

TAKES: 20 MIN. • **MAKES:** 6 SERVINGS

- 1 pkg. (16 oz.) frozen edamame pods
- 2 tsp. kosher salt
- ¾ tsp. ground ginger
- ½ tsp. garlic powder
- ¼ tsp. crushed red pepper flakes

Place edamame in a large saucepan and cover with water. Bring to a boil. Cover and cook until tender, 4-5 minutes; drain. Transfer to a large bowl. Add the seasonings; toss to coat.

1 serving: 52 cal., 2g fat (0 sat. fat), 0 chol., 642mg sod., 5g carb. (1g sugars, 2g fiber), 4g pro.

INSPIRED BY P.F. CHANG'S®
EDAMAME

INSPIRED BY
P.F. CHANG'S®
*HAND-FOLDED
CRAB WONTONS*

INSPIRED BY KFC®

CHILI LIME FRIED CHICKEN

CHILI-LIME CHICKEN WINGS

Who would have guessed that mixing maple syrup, chili sauce and lime juice would make chicken wings taste so good? Family and guests alike will scramble to ensure they get more than one of these utterly delicious wings—so be sure to make extras!

—Taste of Home *Test Kitchen*

PREP: 20 MIN. • **COOK:** 10 MIN./BATCH • **MAKES:** 2 DOZEN

2½ lbs. whole chicken wings
1 cup maple syrup
⅔ cup chili sauce
2 Tbsp. lime juice
2 Tbsp. Dijon mustard
1 cup all-purpose flour
2 tsp. salt
2 tsp. paprika
¼ tsp. pepper
 Oil for deep-fat frying
 Optional: Thinly sliced green onions and lime wedges

1. Cut wings into 3 sections; discard wing tip sections. In a large saucepan, combine syrup, chili sauce, lime juice and mustard. Bring to a boil; cook until liquid is reduced to about 1 cup.

2. Meanwhile, in a large shallow dish, combine flour, salt, paprika and pepper. Add wings a few at a time and toss to coat.

3. In an electric skillet or deep fryer, heat oil to 375°. Fry wings, a few at a time, for 6-8 minutes or until no longer pink, turning once. Drain on paper towels. Transfer wings to a large bowl; add sauce mixture and toss to coat. Serve immediately, with sliced green onions and lime wedges if desired.

Note: Uncooked chicken wing sections (wingettes) may be substituted for whole chicken wings.

1 piece: 142 cal., 8g fat (1g sat. fat), 15mg chol., 198mg sod., 12g carb. (9g sugars, 0 fiber), 5g pro.

MOZZARELLA STICKS

While I always get mozzarella sticks whenever I'm at Olive Garden, sometimes I like to make them at home. My version is baked, not deep-fried, but if you want to hold true to the original, go ahead and drop them into some hot oil.

—*Mary Merchant, Barre, VT*

PREP: 15 MIN. + FREEZING • **BAKE:** 10 MIN. • **MAKES:** 6 SERVINGS

3 Tbsp. all-purpose flour
2 large eggs
1 Tbsp. water
1 cup dry bread crumbs
2½ tsp. Italian seasoning
½ tsp. garlic powder
⅛ tsp. pepper
12 sticks string cheese
   Cooking spray
1 cup marinara or spaghetti sauce, heated

1. Place flour in a shallow bowl. In another shallow bowl, beat eggs and water. In a third shallow bowl, combine the bread crumbs, Italian seasoning, garlic powder and pepper. Coat cheese sticks with flour, then dip in egg mixture and coat with bread crumb mixture. Repeat egg and bread crumb coatings. Cover and freeze for at least 2 hours or overnight.

2. Place on a parchment-lined baking sheet; spray with cooking spray. Bake, uncovered, at 400° for 6-8 minutes or until heated through. Allow to stand for 3-5 minutes before serving. Serve the sticks with marinara or spaghetti sauce for dipping.

2 sticks: 312 cal., 17g fat (10g sat. fat), 116mg chol., 749mg sod., 22g carb. (4g sugars, 1g fiber), 20g pro.

DID YOU KNOW?

You can freeze any leftover mozzarella sticks. Simply let them cool, then transfer to an airtight container. Freeze for up to 3 months, then reheat them the same way you would if they were thawed. The texture of the cheese might be softer than when they were initially cooked.

INSPIRED BY
OLIVE GARDEN®
*MOZZARELLA
STICKS*

INSPIRED BY
PANERA®

*STRAWBERRY
POPPYSEED
SALAD*

SPECIALTY SOUPS, SALADS & SANDWICHES

Mix up mealtime routines with the greatest culinary trio of all time! Soup, salad, sandwich, or maybe all three? You can't go wrong with any of the copycats that follow.

QUESADILLA BURGER

My niece fell in love with the quesadilla burger from Applebee's and challenged me to make it at home. She says I got pretty darned close to the real thing!
—*James Schend, Pleasant Prairie, WI*

PREP: 15 MIN. • **COOK:** 20 MIN. • **MAKES:** 4 SERVINGS

- 1⅓ lbs. ground beef
- ¾ tsp. salt
- ¼ tsp. pepper
- 1 Tbsp. canola oil
- 4 slices pepper jack cheese
- 8 mini flour tortillas
- 2 cups shredded cheddar cheese
- 4 cooked bacon strips, halved
- 4 lettuce leaves
- ½ cup chipotle ranch salad dressing
- ½ cup pico de gallo

1. Shape ground beef into four 5-in.-wide patties. Sprinkle with salt and pepper. In a large skillet, heat oil over medium heat. Add burgers; cook until a thermometer reads 160°, 4-6 minutes on each side. Remove from heat; top with pepper jack cheese. Cover and let stand 5 minutes.

2. Meanwhile, place tortillas on a griddle. Sprinkle ¼ cup cheddar cheese on each tortilla. Cook over low heat until cheese is melted, 1-2 minutes; remove from heat. Top half the tortillas with the burgers, bacon, lettuce, ranch dressing and pico de gallo; top with remaining tortillas, cheese side down.

1 burger: 925 cal., 67g fat (27g sat. fat), 189mg chol., 1640mg sod., 23g carb. (3g sugars, 3g fiber), 53g pro.

HAVE IT YOUR WAY.

If you want to stray from this copycat recipe, you can get creative in a number of ways. You could make your own ranch dressing and mix in a little taco seasoning for added zip. Or, you could make a homemade pico de gallo, which is a terrific way to use garden-fresh tomatoes.

INSPIRED BY
APPLEBEE'S®

*QUESADILLA
BURGER*

INSPIRED BY
OLIVE
GARDEN®
ZUPPA TOSCANA

POTATO, SAUSAGE & KALE SOUP

I let my young son pick out seed packets and he chose kale, which grew like crazy.
This hearty soup helped make good use of it and rivals the Olive Garden's Zuppa Toscana.
—*Michelle Babbie, Malone, NY*

TAKES: 30 MIN. • **MAKES:** 4 SERVINGS

½ lb. bulk pork sausage
1 medium onion, finely chopped
2 tsp. chicken bouillon granules
½ tsp. garlic powder
½ tsp. pepper
2 medium red potatoes,
  cut into ½-in. cubes
2 cups sliced fresh kale
3 cups 2% milk
1 cup heavy whipping cream
1 Tbsp. cornstarch
¼ cup cold water
  Crumbled cooked bacon,
  optional

WHY YOU'LL LOVE IT...

"This is a tasty, fast one-pot meal. My family enjoyed it, and I will make again. Especially great on a cold fall or winter night with a green salad and a crusty bread."
—JGA2595176, TASTEOFHOME.COM

1. In a large saucepan, cook sausage and onion over medium heat 4-6 minutes or until sausage is no longer pink and onion is tender, breaking up sausage into crumbles; drain.
2. Stir in bouillon and the seasonings. Add potatoes, kale, milk and cream; bring to a boil. Reduce heat; simmer, covered, 10-15 minutes or until potatoes are tender.
3. In a small bowl, mix the cornstarch and water until smooth; stir into soup. Return to a boil, stirring constantly; cook and stir 1-2 minutes or until thickened. If desired, top with bacon.

1½ cups: 504 cal., 38g fat (20g sat. fat), 128mg chol., 881mg sod., 26g carb. (12g sugars, 2g fiber), 15g pro.

JALAPENO BURGERS WITH GORGONZOLA

We mixed homemade jalapeno jam into ground beef patties, then topped
the burgers with caramelized onions and tangy Gorgonzola cheese. Fabulous!

—*Becky Mollenkamp, St. Louis, MO*

TAKES: 30 MIN. • **MAKES:** 4 SERVINGS

1 Tbsp. canola oil
1 tsp. butter
1 medium onion, halved
  and thinly sliced
  Dash salt
  Dash sugar

BURGERS
⅓ cup jalapeno pepper jelly
½ tsp. salt
¼ tsp. pepper
1 lb. ground beef
4 hamburger buns, split
  and toasted
2 Tbsp. crumbled Gorgonzola
  cheese
  Thinly sliced jalapeno pepper,
  optional

1. In a small skillet, heat oil and butter over medium heat. Add onion, salt and sugar; cook and stir until onion is softened, 3-4 minutes. Reduce heat to medium-low; cook until deep golden brown, stirring occasionally, 4-6 minutes.

2. In a large bowl, mix jelly, salt and pepper. Add beef; mix lightly but thoroughly. Shape into four ½-in- thick patties.

3. Grill burgers, covered, over medium heat or broil 4 in. from heat until a thermometer reads 160°, 4-5 minutes on each side. Serve on buns with caramelized onion, cheese and, if desired, jalapeno slices.

1 burger: 460 cal., 20g fat (7g sat. fat), 76mg chol., 669mg sod., 43g carb. (18g sugars, 2g fiber), 25g pro.

INSPIRED BY
RED ROBIN®

*BURNIN' LOVE
BURGER*

**INSPIRED BY
UNO PIZZERIA & GRILL®**

*WHISKY BBQ
CHICKEN SANDWICH*

CINNAMON WHISKEY BBQ CHICKEN MELT

I re-created this sandwich from the Uno Pizzeria & Grill menu. Make the sauce ahead so the sandwiches will come together quickly when the craving hits! I make my sandwiches in a panini press set to medium.

—*Jolene Martinelli, Fremont, NH*

TAKES: 30 MIN. • **MAKES:** 2 SERVINGS

4   frozen breaded
    chicken tenders
3   Tbsp. barbecue sauce
2   tsp. whiskey
¼   tsp. ground cinnamon
4   slices sourdough bread
4   slices cheddar cheese
4   cooked bacon strips
2   Tbsp. ranch salad dressing
4   tsp. butter, softened

1. Prepare chicken tenders according to package directions. Meanwhile, stir together barbecue sauce, whiskey and cinnamon.

2. Top 2 slices of bread with half the cheddar cheese; add bacon. Place chicken tenders on top of bacon. Drizzle with barbecue sauce and ranch; top with remaining cheese. Top with remaining bread. Spread outsides of sandwiches with butter.

3. In a skillet over medium heat, toast sandwiches until cheese is melted and outside is golden brown, 2-3 minutes on each side.

1 sandwich: 691 cal., 41g fat (19g sat. fat), 102mg chol., 1626mg sod., 50g carb. (13g sugars, 2g fiber), 29g pro.

TEQUILA-LIME STEAK SALAD

This NutriFit copycat recipe has become one of my family's Fourth of July favorites. The adults can make margaritas from the rest of the tequila!
—*Laura Wilhelm, West Hollywood, CA*

PREP: 15 MIN. + MARINATING • **GRILL:** 10 MIN. • **MAKES:** 6 SERVINGS

¾ cup plus 1 Tbsp. lime juice, divided
¾ cup blanco tequila
2 Tbsp. garlic powder
1 Tbsp. ground cumin
1 Tbsp. Montreal steak seasoning
1 Tbsp. dried oregano
½ tsp. pepper
⅛ tsp. crushed red pepper flakes
2 lbs. beef flank steak
1 pkg. (9 to 10 oz.) hearts of romaine salad mix
3 Tbsp. olive oil
1 pint rainbow cherry tomatoes, halved
Optional: Cotija cheese and lime wedges

1. In a large bowl, whisk together ¾ cup lime juice, tequila, garlic powder, cumin, steak seasoning, oregano, pepper and red pepper flakes. Place steak in a shallow dish; add tequila mixture and turn to coat. Refrigerate, covered, 8 hours or overnight, turning once.

2. Drain beef, discarding marinade; pat dry. Grill, covered, over direct medium-high heat, turning once, until desired degree of doneness (for medium-rare, a thermometer should read 135°; medium, 140°; medium-well, 145°), 10-15 minutes. Place beef on cutting board; cover and let rest 5-10 minutes. Thinly slice steak across the grain.

3. Place salad mix on serving platter; drizzle with olive oil and remaining 1 Tbsp. lime juice. Place steak over romaine; top with tomatoes and if desired, cotija cheese and lime wedges.

4 oz. cooked steak with 1½ cups salad: 257 cal., 11g fat (5g sat. fat), 72mg chol., 243mg sod., 8g carb. (2g sugars, 2g fiber), 31g pro.
Diabetic exchanges: 4 lean meat, 1½ fat, 1 vegetable.

INSPIRED BY
NUTRIFIT

*TEQUILA & LIME
MARINATED
STEAK SALAD*

INSPIRED BY
PANERA®

*PESTO CHICKEN
SANDWICH*

CHICKEN PESTO SANDWICHES

Years ago I had a pesto chicken sandwich at Panera and fell in love.
I haven't seen it on that menu for a long time so I had to create my own version.

—Colleen Sturma, Milwaukee, WI

TAKES: 30 MIN. • **MAKES:** 6 SERVINGS

6 boneless skinless chicken breast halves (6 oz. each)
¾ cup prepared pesto, divided
½ tsp. salt
¼ tsp. pepper
1 jar (12 oz.) roasted sweet red peppers, drained
6 ciabatta buns, split and toasted
¼ lb. fresh mozzarella cheese, cut into 6 slices

1. Flatten chicken to ¼-in. thickness. Spread 1 Tbsp. pesto over each chicken breast; sprinkle with salt and pepper. Grill chicken, covered, over medium heat until no longer pink, 3-5 minutes on each side.

2. Spread 3 Tbsp. pesto over bun bottoms; layer with red peppers, chicken and cheese. Spread remaining pesto over bun tops; place over cheese.

1 sandwich: 498 cal., 22g fat (6g sat. fat), 111mg chol., 1026mg sod., 27g carb. (6g sugars, 1g fiber), 43g pro.

DID YOU KNOW?

If you are unable to find fresh mozzarella, you can use regular mozzarella or provolone slices. However, we recommend going out of your way to pick up some fresh mozzarella, because it makes all the difference!

COPYCAT SOUTHWEST CHICKEN SALAD

My husband and I loved this salad the first time we tried it at Applebee's. After eating it three times, my husband asked for information on the ingredients in the dressing. The waitress told us, so I went home and worked on a version we think tastes just as delicious.

—*Pamela Shank, Parkersburg, WV*

TAKES: 30 MIN. • **MAKES:** 2 SERVINGS

⅓ cup chopped red onion
¼ cup pickled jalapeno slices, chopped
¼ cup coleslaw salad dressing
1 Tbsp. juice from pickled jalapeno slices
1 Tbsp. lime juice
2 boneless skinless chicken breast halves (6 oz. each)
¼ cup frozen corn
3 cups chopped romaine
¼ cup chopped sweet red pepper
¼ cup chopped seeded tomatoes
¼ cup canned black beans, rinsed and drained
½ cup shredded cheddar cheese
½ cup tri-color tortilla strips

1. Place the first 5 ingredients in a jar with a tight-fitting lid; shake well. Refrigerate until serving.

2. Place chicken on oiled grill rack. Grill, covered, over medium heat or broil 3 in. from heat until a thermometer reads 165°, 5-7 minutes on each side. Let stand 5 minutes before slicing. Meanwhile, prepare corn according to package directions.

3. Divide romaine between 2 salad bowls. Arrange chicken over the romaine; top with corn, red pepper, tomatoes and beans. Sprinkle with cheese and tortilla strips. Shake dressing again; drizzle over salads. Serve immediately.

1 salad: 557 cal., 26g fat (8g sat. fat), 132mg chol., 826mg sod., 33g carb. (9g sugars, 4g fiber), 45g pro.

INSPIRED BY
APPLEBEE'S®

*SOUTHWESTERN
CHICKEN SALAD*

INSPIRED BY ARBY'S®
BEEF & CHEDDAR

BEEF & CHEDDAR SLIDERS

These delicious sliders are made from deli roast beef and a copycat Arby's sauce. The recipe is a quick weeknight meal and an amazing replica of the wonderful beef and cheddar sandwich from Arby's. If you like your sandwiches really cheesy, go ahead and add another layer on top of the beef before baking.
—*Claudia Lamascolo, Melbourne, FL*

PREP: 15 MIN. • **BAKE:** 30 MIN. • **MAKES:** 6 SERVINGS

1 pkg. (12 oz.) Hawaiian sweet rolls
14 oz. thinly sliced deli roast beef
½ cup barbecue sauce
6 slices sharp cheddar cheese
¼ cup butter, cubed
2 Tbsp. brown sugar
2 tsp. Worcestershire sauce
2 tsp. prepared mustard
1½ tsp. dried minced onion or poppy seeds
½ tsp. garlic powder

1. Preheat oven to 350°. Without separating rolls, cut the package of rolls in half horizontally; arrange bottom halves in a greased 11x7-in. baking dish. In a bowl, combine roast beef and barbecue sauce. Top with cheese slices. Replace top halves of rolls.

2. In a small skillet, melt butter over medium heat. Whisk in the brown sugar, Worcestershire sauce, mustard, dried minced onion and garlic powder. Cook and stir until sugar is dissolved; drizzle over the sandwiches.

3. Cover and bake 25 minutes. Uncover; bake until golden brown, 5-10 minutes longer.

2 sliders: 335 cal., 20g fat (13g sat. fat), 78mg chol., 587mg sod., 25g carb. (12g sugars, 1g fiber), 16g pro.

DRIVE-THRU CHILI

I don't eat a lot of fast food—but when I do, I try to pick things that are fairly healthy.
I found that Wendy's chili is one of the healthiest items on its menu. So when I needed
to bring chili to a potluck, I tried to re-create Wendy's recipe, and I think it got it pretty close.

—Margo Zoerner, Pleasant Prairie, WI

PREP: 20 MIN. • **COOK:** 1 HOUR • **MAKES:** 20 SERVINGS (5 QT.)

2½ lbs. ground beef
2 cups chopped onion
1 cup chopped celery
3 Tbsp. chili powder
1 Tbsp. ground cumin
1 tsp. pepper
1 can (4 oz.) chopped
   green chiles
1 garlic clove, minced
1 can (46 oz.) tomato juice
4 cups V8 juice
1 can (28 oz.) diced tomatoes,
   undrained
2 cans (16 oz. each) kidney beans,
   rinsed and drained
2 cans (16 oz. each) pink beans
   or pinto beans, rinsed and
   drained
   Optional: Sour cream,
   cubed avocado, shredded
   cheddar cheese and
   sliced jalapeno pepper

1. In a large Dutch oven, cook beef over medium heat until no longer pink; drain. Continue to cook until beef is browned, 4-5 minutes longer. Add the onion and celery; cook until tender. Stir in chili powder, cumin and pepper; cook 1 minute. Add the green chiles and garlic; cook 1 minute longer.

2. Stir in juices and tomatoes. Bring to a boil. Reduce heat; simmer, uncovered, for 20 minutes. Add beans and simmer 20 minutes longer or until thickened to desired consistency. If desired, serve with sour cream, avocado, cheese and jalapeno slices.

Freeze option: Freeze cooled chili in freezer containers. To use, partially thaw in refrigerator overnight. Heat through in a saucepan, stirring occasionally; add a little water if necessary.

Note: This recipe was tested with Goya Pink Beans (Habichuelas Rosadas).

1 cup: 225 cal., 7g fat (3g sat. fat), 35mg chol., 595mg sod., 23g carb. (7g sugars, 6g fiber), 17g pro.

INSPIRED BY
P.F. CHANG'S®
LETTUCE WRAPS

COPYCAT P.F. CHANG'S LETTUCE WRAPS

Not only do these savory wraps taste as if they came from a restaurant, but they're also a fun way to jazz up your weeknight-meal routine. They come together fast—and you can save even more time by using last night's cooked chicken.

—Kendra Doss, Colorado Springs, CO

TAKES: 25 MIN. • **MAKES:** 6 SERVINGS

1 Tbsp. plus 1½ tsp. peanut oil, divided
1½ lbs. boneless skinless chicken breasts, cubed
¾ cup chopped fresh mushrooms
1 can (8 oz.) water chestnuts, drained and diced
1 Tbsp. minced fresh gingerroot
2 Tbsp. rice vinegar
2 Tbsp. reduced-sodium teriyaki sauce
1 Tbsp. reduced-sodium soy sauce
½ tsp. garlic powder
¼ tsp. crushed red pepper flakes
½ cup julienned green onions
12 Bibb or Boston lettuce leaves

1. In a large nonstick skillet, heat 1 Tbsp. oil over medium-high heat. Add chicken. Cook and stir for 3 minutes; drain. Add mushrooms, water chestnuts and ginger; cook until chicken is no longer pink, 4-6 minutes longer. Drain and set aside.

2. In a small bowl, whisk vinegar, teriyaki sauce, soy sauce, garlic powder, red pepper flakes and remaining 1½ tsp. oil. Stir in onions and chicken mixture.

3. Spoon onto lettuce leaves. If desired, fold sides of lettuce over filling and roll up.

2 wraps: 232 cal., 13g fat (3g sat. fat), 75mg chol., 641mg sod., 11g carb. (5g sugars, 2g fiber), 20g pro. **Diabetic exchanges:** 3 lean meat, ½ starch, ½ fat.

COPYCAT CHICKEN SALAD

Inspired by Chick-fil-A chicken salad, this recipe is incredibly easy to make, and your family will love it. The sweet pickle relish gives it that signature taste. I like to use a thick crusty oat bread.

—Julie Peterson, Crofton, MD

TAKES: 20 MIN. • **MAKES:** 2 SERVINGS

½ cup reduced-fat mayonnaise
⅓ cup sweet pickle relish
⅓ cup finely chopped celery
½ tsp. sugar
¼ tsp. salt
¼ tsp. pepper
1 hard-boiled large egg, cooled and minced
2 cups chopped cooked chicken breast
4 slices whole wheat bread, toasted
2 romaine leaves

Mix the first 7 ingredients; stir in chicken. Line 2 slices of toast with lettuce. Top with chicken salad and remaining toast slices.

1 sandwich: 651 cal., 29g fat (5g sat. fat), 222mg chol., 1386mg sod., 45g carb. (18g sugars, 4g fiber), 51g pro.

WHY YOU'LL LOVE IT...

"We love this chicken salad. Easy to make, perfect for lunch. Sometimes we have it for a light supper with crackers and fruit."
—DEBGLASS11, TASTEOFHOME.COM

INSPIRED BY
CHICK-FIL-A®
*CHICKEN
SALAD*

INSPIRED BY
KFC®
COLESLAW

COPYCAT COLESLAW

We love going to KFC. Although we enjoy the chicken, we actually go for the coleslaw—
and we'll buy several pints at a time! Although I make different versions of coleslaw, it took me quite
a few years before getting this recipe right. If you are in a hurry, pick up a bag of shredded slaw mix.

—Donna Gribbins, Shelbyville, KY

PREP: 20 MIN. + CHILLING • **MAKES:** 8 SERVINGS

½ cup buttermilk
½ cup mayonnaise
⅓ cup sugar
2 Tbsp. lemon juice
4½ tsp. white vinegar
1 tsp. salt
½ tsp. pepper
1 lb. finely chopped cabbage
    (about 8 cups)
2 medium carrots, finely
    chopped (about 2 cups)
3 Tbsp. grated onion

In a large bowl, whisk the first 7 ingredients until combined. Add the remaining ingredients; toss to coat. Refrigerate, covered, at least 2 hours and up to 3 days before serving.

¾ cup: 160 cal., 10g fat (2g sat. fat), 6mg chol., 421mg sod., 16g carb. (13g sugars, 3g fiber), 2g pro.

COPY THAT!

It is completely normal for the cabbage to release water when mixed with the other ingredients in this recipe. This helps contribute to the dressing, and evenly coats the coleslaw. If you don't like so much liquid, you can easily drain it off before serving. Better yet, serve this coleslaw with a slotted spoon.

PAT'S KING OF STEAKS PHILLY CHEESESTEAK

This ultimate cheesesteak, an iconic sandwich in Philly, is a best-seller at
Pat's King of Steaks Restaurant. Patrons praise its thinly cut beef and crusty Italian rolls.
—*Frank Olivieri, Philadelphia, PA*

TAKES: 20 MIN. • **MAKES:** 4 SERVINGS

1 large onion, sliced
½ lb. sliced fresh mushrooms, optional
1 small green pepper, sliced, optional
1 small sweet red pepper, sliced, optional
6 Tbsp. canola oil, divided
1½ lbs. beef ribeye steaks, thinly sliced
4 crusty Italian rolls, split
Process cheese sauce
Ketchup, optional

1. In a large skillet, saute the onion and, if desired, mushrooms and peppers in 3 Tbsp. oil until tender. Remove and keep warm. In the same pan, saute beef in remaining oil in batches for 45-60 seconds or until meat reaches desired doneness.

2. On each roll bottom, layer the beef, onion mixture, cheese and, if desired, ketchup. Replace tops.

1 sandwich: 714 cal., 49g fat (12g sat. fat), 101mg chol., 299mg sod., 31g carb. (3g sugars, 2g fiber), 36g pro.

INSPIRED BY
PAT'S KING OF STEAKS®
MUSHROOM PEPPER STEAK

INSPIRED BY
CHIPOTLE
MEXICAN GRILL®

*CHIPOTLE HONEY
VINAIGRETTE*

HONEY CHIPOTLE VINAIGRETTE

We've all been there. It's 7 p.m. and you're at home with a sudden craving for Chipotle.
You don't feel like going all the way to Chipotle—it doesn't have a drive-thru anyway— and delivery feels too slow.
What's a hungry person to do? You make an at-home Chipotle salad complete with a copycat version
of its Chipotle Honey Vinaigrette! It's one of our favorite homemade salad dressings.

—Lauren Habermehl, Pewaukee, WI

TAKES: 15 MIN. • **MAKES:** 1 CUP

⅓ cup red wine vinegar
3 Tbsp. honey
1 chipotle pepper in adobo sauce
1½ tsp. adobo sauce
1 tsp. garlic powder
1 tsp. ground cumin
¾ tsp. salt
½ tsp. dried oregano
¼ tsp. pepper
½ cup extra virgin olive oil

In a blender or food processor, combine the first 9 ingredients; puree until smooth. With the motor running, slowly drizzle in olive oil.
2 Tbsp.: 152 cal., 14g fat (2g sat. fat), 0 chol., 253mg sod., 8g carb. (7g sugars, 0 fiber), 0 pro.

STRAWBERRY KALE SALAD

This fresh, zingy salad is super easy and just like the one I get at Culver's!
The sliced strawberries and fresh mint give it an extra-summery feel, and
crumbled bacon and toasted almonds add the perfect amount of crunch.

—Luanne Asta, Hampton Bays, NY

TAKES: 25 MIN. • **MAKES:** 10 SERVINGS

½ cup olive oil
⅓ cup cider vinegar
1 tsp. honey
¼ tsp. salt
⅛ tsp. pepper
1 bunch kale (about 12 oz.), trimmed and chopped (about 14 cups)
2 cups sliced fresh strawberries
¾ lb. bacon strips, cooked and crumbled
¼ cup minced fresh mint
1 cup crumbled feta cheese
¼ cup slivered almonds, toasted

1. For dressing, whisk together the first 5 ingredients.
2. To serve, place the kale, strawberries, bacon and mint in a large bowl; toss with dressing. Sprinkle with cheese and almonds.
Note: To toast nuts, bake in a shallow pan in a 350°; oven for 5-10 minutes or cook in a skillet over low heat until lightly browned, stirring occasionally.
1⅓ cups: 231 cal., 19g fat (4g sat. fat), 18mg chol., 399mg sod., 8g carb. (2g sugars, 2g fiber), 8g pro.

INSPIRED BY CULVER'S®
STRAWBERRY FIELDS SALAD

COPYCAT FRIED CHICKEN SANDWICH

After trying all the major fast food chain's chicken sandwiches, I decided to come up with my own version. I know everyone says theirs is better than the original, but mine really is!

—Ralph Jones, San Diego, CA

PREP: 15 MIN. + MARINATING • **COOK:** 20 MIN./BATCH • **MAKES:** 6 SERVINGS

3 boneless skinless chicken breast halves (6 oz. each)
¾ cup buttermilk
2 tsp. hot pepper sauce
2 large eggs, beaten
2 cups all-purpose flour
1 Tbsp. plus 1 tsp. garlic powder
1 Tbsp. each onion powder and paprika
2 tsp. pepper
1 tsp. salt
⅓ cup canola oil
6 brioche hamburger buns, split
Optional: Shredded lettuce, sliced tomatoes, pickle slices, onion slices, mayonnaise

1. Cut each chicken breast horizontally in half; place in a large bowl. Add buttermilk and hot sauce; toss to coat. Refrigerate, covered, 8 hours or overnight.

2. Preheat air fryer to 400°. Stir eggs into chicken mixture. In a shallow dish, whisk flour, garlic powder, onion powder, paprika, pepper and salt. Remove chicken from buttermilk mixture. Dredge chicken in flour mixture, firmly patting to help coating adhere. Repeat, dipping chicken again in the buttermilk mixture and then dredging in the flour mixture.

3. Place chicken on a wire rack over a baking sheet. Refrigerate, uncovered, for 30 minutes. Using a pastry brush, lightly dab both sides of chicken with oil until no dry breading remains.

4. In batches, arrange chicken in a single layer on greased tray in air-fryer basket. Cook until a thermometer reads 165° and coating is golden brown and crispy, 7-8 minutes on each side. Remove chicken; keep warm. Toast buns in air fryer until golden brown, 2-3 minutes. Top bun bottoms with chicken. If desired, add optional toppings. Replace bun tops.

Note: In our testing, we find that cook times vary dramatically between brands of air fryers. As a result, we give wider than normal ranges on suggested cook times. Begin checking at the first time listed and adjust as needed.

1 sandwich: 384 cal., 17g fat (3g sat. fat), 136mg chol., 777mg sod., 31g carb. (8g sugars, 3g fiber), 26g pro.

HAVE IT YOUR WAY.

Making spicy mayo can be as simple as mixing together mayonnaise and your favorite hot pepper sauce. Adjust it to whatever heat level you prefer.

INSPIRED BY
POPEYES®
*CLASSIC CHICKEN
SANDWICH*

INSPIRED BY PANERA®

STRAWBERRY POPPYSEED SALAD

SUMMER STRAWBERRY SALAD

I love the Strawberry Poppyseed Salad at Panera but can't always make it to the restaurant. That's why I created my own version. It's quick, delicious and ready when I want it.

—*Diane Marie Sahley, Lakewood, OH*

TAKES: 15 MIN. • **MAKES:** 4 SERVINGS

1 pkg. (10 oz.) romaine salad mix (about 8 cups)
1 lb. sliced cooked chicken
1½ cups sliced fresh strawberries
1 cup pineapple tidbits, drained
½ cup mandarin oranges, drained
½ cup fresh blueberries
½ cup chopped pecans
½ cup poppy seed salad dressing

Arrange romaine on 4 serving plates. Top with chicken, strawberries, pineapple, mandarin oranges and blueberries. Sprinkle with pecans. Drizzle with dressing.

2 cups: 557 cal., 31g fat (5g sat. fat), 111mg chol., 329mg sod., 34g carb. (25g sugars, 5g fiber), 37g pro.

INSPIRED BY
FOGO DE CHAO®

*LAMB CHOP RACK
WITH MINT JELLY*

COPYCAT ENTREES

It's easier than ever to enjoy menu favorites without leaving home or spending a lot of cash. Simply whip up these mouthwatering mains when a restaurant craving hits.

COPYCAT KFC FRIED CHICKEN

This fried chicken can be served hot or pulled out of the fridge the next day as leftovers. Either way, folks love it.
—*Jeanne Schnitzler, Lima, MT*

PREP: 15 MIN. • **COOK:** 15 MIN./BATCH • **MAKES:** 12 SERVINGS

4 cups all-purpose flour, divided
2 Tbsp. garlic salt
1 Tbsp. paprika
3 tsp. pepper, divided
2½ tsp. poultry seasoning
2 large eggs
1½ cups water
1 tsp. salt
2 broiler/fryer chickens
   (3½ to 4 lbs. each), cut up
   Oil for deep-fat frying

1. In a large shallow dish, combine 2⅔ cups flour, garlic salt, paprika, 2½ tsp. pepper and poultry seasoning. In another shallow dish, beat the eggs and 1½ cups water; add salt and the remaining 1⅓ cups flour and ½ tsp. pepper. Dip chicken in egg mixture, then place in flour mixture, a few pieces at a time. Turn to coat.
2. In a deep-fat fryer, heat oil to 375°. Fry chicken, several pieces at a time, until chicken is golden brown and juices run clear, about 7-8 minutes on each side. Drain on paper towels.

5 oz. cooked chicken: 543 cal., 33g fat (7g sat. fat), 137mg chol., 798mg sod., 17g carb. (0 sugars, 1g fiber), 41g pro.

COPY THAT!

A thrifty alternative to purchased garlic salt is to mix up your own. Just combine 1 tsp. garlic powder with 3 tsp. table salt or other fine-grained salt. The ratio works the same for onion salt, too.

INSPIRED BY
KFC®

ORIGINAL RECIPE
CHICKEN

**INSPIRED BY
BURGER KING®**

*STUFFED STEAKHOUSE
BURGER*

KING BURGERS

My husband is a grill master, and we make up recipes together. The sauce for this juicy burger tastes even better when it's been refrigerated overnight.

—Mary Potter, Sterling Heights, MI

TAKES: 30 MIN. • **MAKES:** 6 SERVINGS

2 Tbsp. butter
¼ cup mayonnaise
2 Tbsp. prepared horseradish
2 Tbsp. Dijon mustard
⅛ tsp. salt
⅛ tsp. pepper

BURGERS

1½ lbs. ground beef
⅓ cup beef broth
2½ tsp. hamburger seasoning, divided
6 hamburger buns, split
3 Tbsp. butter, softened
   Optional: Shredded lettuce, sliced tomato and red onion

1. Cut 2 Tbsp. butter into 6 slices, let remaining butter soften. Place slices in a single layer on a small plate; freeze until firm. For sauce, in a small bowl, mix the mayonnaise, horseradish, mustard, salt and pepper until blended.

2. In a large bowl, combine beef, broth and 1½ tsp. hamburger seasoning; mix lightly but thoroughly. Shape into 6 patties. Place a butter slice in the center of each; shape beef around butter, forming ¾-in.-thick patties. Sprinkle the patties with the remaining 1 tsp. hamburger seasoning.

3. Grill burgers, covered, over medium heat 5-7 minutes on each side or until a thermometer reads 160°. Spread buns with softened butter. Grill buns over medium heat, cut side down, for 30-60 seconds or until toasted. Serve burgers on buns with sauce and toppings.

Freeze option: Place patties on a foil-lined baking sheet; wrap and freeze until firm. Remove from pan and transfer to a freezer container; return to freezer. To use, cook frozen patties as directed, increasing time as necessary for a thermometer to read 160°.

1 burger: 482 cal., 32g fat (12g sat. fat), 99mg chol., 822mg sod., 23g carb. (3g sugars, 1g fiber), 25g pro.

FISH & FRIES

Dine as though you're in a traditional British pub. These moist fish fillets from the oven
have a fuss-free coating that's healthy but just as crunchy and golden as the deep-fried kind.
Simply seasoned and baked, the crispy fries are perfect on the side.

—Janice Mitchell, Aurora, CO

PREP: 10 MIN. • **BAKE:** 35 MIN. • **MAKES:** 4 SERVINGS

1   lb. potatoes (about 2 medium)
2   Tbsp. olive oil
¼   tsp. pepper

FISH
⅓   cup all-purpose flour
¼   tsp. pepper
1   large egg
2   Tbsp. water
⅔   cup crushed cornflakes
1   Tbsp. grated Parmesan cheese
⅛   tsp. cayenne pepper
1   lb. haddock or cod fillets
    Tartar sauce, optional

1. Preheat oven to 425°. Peel and cut potatoes lengthwise into ½-in.-thick slices; cut slices into ½-in.-thick sticks.

2. In a large bowl, toss potatoes with oil and pepper. Transfer to a 15x10x1-in. baking pan coated with cooking spray. Bake, uncovered, 25-30 minutes or until golden brown and crisp, stirring once.

3. Meanwhile, in a shallow bowl, mix flour and pepper. In another shallow bowl, whisk egg with water. In a third bowl, toss cornflakes with cheese and cayenne. Dip fish in flour mixture to coat both sides; shake off excess. Dip in egg mixture, then in cornflake mixture, patting to help coating adhere.

4. Place on a baking sheet coated with cooking spray. Bake roughly 10-12 minutes or until fish just begins to flake easily with a fork. Serve with potatoes and, if desired, tartar sauce.

1 serving: 376 cal., 9g fat (2g sat. fat), 120mg chol., 228mg sod., 44g carb. (3g sugars, 2g fiber), 28g pro. **Diabetic exchanges:** 3 starch, 3 lean meat, 1½ fat.

**INSPIRED BY
LONG JOHN
SILVER'S®**

*PACIFIC COD
AND FRIES*

**INSPIRED BY
FOGO DE CHAO®**

*LAMB CHOP RACK
WITH MINT JELLY*

GRILLED LAMB WITH MINT-PEPPER JELLY

It's not on the menu, but if you go to Fogo de Chao, make sure you ask for the mint jelly they serve with their rack of lamb. It's divine! This is my version, using zippy jalapeno pepper jelly. It's my surefire way of getting people who aren't typically fans of lamb to enjoy it.

—*Lori Stefanishion, Drumheller, AB*

PREP: 15 MIN. + MARINATING • **GRILL:** 30 MIN. + STANDING • **MAKES:** 4 SERVINGS

2 racks of lamb (1½ lbs. each), trimmed
3 Tbsp. Greek seasoning
¼ cup balsamic vinegar
¼ cup olive oil
2 Tbsp. lemon juice
2 Tbsp. soy sauce
3 garlic cloves, minced
½ cup fresh mint leaves, minced
½ cup mild jalapeno pepper jelly
1 Tbsp. hot water
Chopped fresh oregano

1. Rub lamb with Greek seasoning. Refrigerate, covered, 2 hours. In a shallow bowl, whisk vinegar, oil, lemon juice, soy sauce and garlic until combined. Add lamb and turn to coat. Refrigerate, covered, 4-6 hours or overnight, turning once or twice.

2. In a small bowl, mix mint, jelly, and hot water until combined. Refrigerate, covered, until serving.

3. Drain lamb, discarding marinade in dish. Cover rib ends of lamb with foil. Grill, covered, on an oiled rack, over direct medium-high heat 2 minutes on each side. Turn; move to indirect heat. Cook, covered, until meat reaches the desired doneness (for medium-rare, a thermometer should read 135°; medium, 140°; medium-well, 145°), 25-30 minutes longer. Let stand 10 minutes before serving with sauce; sprinkle with fresh oregano and additional fresh mint.

½ rack with 4 Tbsp. sauce: 471 cal., 24g fat (7g sat. fat), 99mg chol., 1841mg sod., 33g carb. (24g sugars, 1g fiber), 31g pro.

SHRIMP TEMPURA

One of my go-to dishes at a local Chinese restaurant is their shrimp tempura. It's crispy, delicate and oh-so delicious.
—Sarah Tramonte, Milwaukee, WI

PREP: 15 MIN. • **COOK:** 20 MIN. • **MAKES:** 26 SERVINGS

¾ cup all-purpose flour
6 Tbsp. cornstarch
2¼ Tbsp. baking soda
½ tsp. salt
¾ cold cup club soda
1 lb. uncooked shrimp (26-30 per lb.), peeled and deveined
Oil for deep-fat frying
Sweet chili sauce, optional

1. In a large bowl, combine the first 4 ingredients. Stir in the cold club soda until combined; mixture will be lumpy. Using a paring knife, cut small slits along the inside of the shrimp to allow it to lie flat without curling up.

2. In an electric skillet or deep-fat fryer, heat oil to 375°. Dip shrimp into batter, then directly into hot oil. Fry shrimp, a few at a time, for 1-2 minutes, or until golden brown. Drain on paper towels. If desired, serve with sweet chili sauce.

1 shrimp: 47 cal., 2g fat (0 sat. fat), 21mg chol., 394mg sod., 5g carb. (0 sugars, 0 fiber), 3g pro.

DID YOU KNOW?

Tempura is a popular Japanese dish where seafood is battered and deep-fried. Lots of cooks use the batter and frying method for vegetable tempura, too. Try broccoli, cauliflower or even large pieces of red or green pepper.

**INSPIRED BY
PANDA EXPRESS®**
FRESH TEMPURA SHRIMP

INSPIRED BY WENDY'S®
CHICKEN TENDERS

SEASONED CHICKEN STRIPS

I made these crisp chicken strips for my kids, but they're tasty enough for company, too.
They're juicy and flavorful and would also be a wonderful salad topper.
—*Becky Oliver, Fairplay, CO*

TAKES: 25 MIN. • **MAKES:** 4 SERVINGS

⅓ cup egg substitute or 1 large egg
1 Tbsp. prepared mustard
1 garlic clove, minced
¾ cup dry bread crumbs
2 tsp. dried basil
1 tsp. paprika
½ tsp. salt
¼ tsp. pepper
1 lb. chicken tenderloins

1. Preheat oven to 400°. In a shallow bowl, whisk together egg substitute, mustard and garlic. In another shallow bowl, toss bread crumbs with seasonings. Dip chicken in egg mixture, then coat with crumb mixture.

2. Place on a baking sheet coated with cooking spray. Bake until golden brown and chicken is no longer pink, 10-15 minutes.

3 oz. cooked chicken: 194 cal., 2g fat (0 sat. fat), 56mg chol., 518mg sod., 14g carb. (1g sugars, 1g fiber), 31g pro. **Diabetic exchanges:** 3 lean meat, 1 starch.

AIR-FRYER ROTISSERIE CHICKEN

This air-fryer whole chicken is so crispy yet succulent, just like the rotisserie chickens you get at Boston Market. I serve it straight up, but you can also shred it and add it to tacos, soups, pasta salads and so much more.

—*Dawn Parker, Surrey, BC*

PREP: 5 MIN. • **COOK:** 65 MIN. + STANDING • **MAKES:** 6 SERVINGS

1 broiler/fryer chicken (3 to 4 lbs.)
1 Tbsp. olive oil
2 tsp. seasoned salt

Preheat air fryer to 350°. Brush outside of chicken with olive oil and sprinkle with seasoned salt. Place chicken, breast side down, on tray in air-fryer basket; cook 30 minutes. Flip the chicken and cook until a thermometer inserted in thickest part of thigh reads 170°-175°, 35-40 minutes longer. Remove chicken; let stand 15 minutes before carving.

Note: In our testing, we find cook times vary dramatically between brands of air fryers. As a result, we give wider than normal ranges on suggested cook times. Begin checking at the first time listed and adjust as needed.

5 oz. cooked chicken: 313 cal., 19g fat (5g sat. fat), 104mg chol., 596mg sod., 0 carb. (0 sugars, 0 fiber), 33g pro.

COPY THAT!

This recipe calls for a 3- or 4-pound chicken, which should fit nicely an air fryer with a 5-qt. capacity (or larger). If your chicken is too big for your air fryer, you can cut the chicken into pieces and adjust the cooking time accordingly.

INSPIRED BY
BOSTON MARKET®
WHOLE CHICKEN

INSPIRED BY
CRACKER
BARREL®

U.S. FARM-RAISED
CATFISH

SKILLET-GRILLED CATFISH

You can use this recipe with any thick fish fillet, but I suggest catfish or haddock. The Cajun flavor is great.

—*Traci Wynne, Denver, PA*

TAKES: 25 MIN. • **MAKES:** 4 SERVINGS

¼ cup all-purpose flour
¼ cup cornmeal
1 tsp. onion powder
1 tsp. dried basil
½ tsp. garlic salt
½ tsp. dried thyme
¼ to ½ tsp. white pepper
¼ to ½ tsp. cayenne pepper
¼ to ½ tsp. pepper
4 catfish fillets (6 to 8 oz. each)
¼ cup butter
  Optional: Lemon wedges and minced fresh parsley

1. In a large shallow dish, combine the first 9 ingredients. Add catfish, 1 fillet at a time, and turn to coat.
2. Place a large cast-iron skillet on a grill rack over medium-high heat. Melt butter in the skillet; add the catfish in batches, if necessary. Grill, covered, until fish just begins to flake easily with a fork, 5-10 minutes on each side. If desired, serve with lemon wedges and fresh parsley.

1 fillet: 222 cal., 15g fat (8g sat. fat), 51mg chol., 366mg sod., 14g carb. (0 sugars, 1g fiber), 8g pro.

WHY YOU'LL LOVE IT...

"I cooked this fish on the stovetop in a cast-iron skillet, not on a grill rack. It turned out crispy, flaky and delicious."
—CYNANDTOM, TASTEOFHOME.COM

SMOTHERED CHICKEN

I top tender chicken breasts with mushrooms, bacon, green onions
and cheese for a quick, comforting meal that's become a family favorite.
—*Penny Walton, Westerville, OH*

TAKES: 20 MIN. • **MAKES:** 4 SERVINGS

4   boneless skinless chicken
    breast halves (5 oz. each)
¼   tsp. seasoned salt
¼   tsp. garlic powder
3   tsp. canola oil, divided
1   cup sliced fresh mushrooms
1   cup shredded Mexican cheese
    blend
4   green onions, chopped
6   bacon strips, cooked and
    chopped

1. Pound chicken breasts to ¼-in. thickness. Sprinkle with the seasonings.

2. In a large nonstick skillet, heat 1 tsp. oil over medium-high heat; saute mushrooms until tender, 2-3 minutes. Remove from pan.

3. In same pan, cook chicken in remaining 2 tsp. oil until bottoms are browned, about 4 minutes. Turn chicken; top with mushrooms and remaining ingredients. Cook, covered, until chicken is no longer pink, 4-5 minutes.

1 chicken breast half: 363 cal., 21g fat (7g sat. fat), 116mg chol., 555mg sod., 3g carb. (1g sugars, 1g fiber), 40g pro.

INSPIRED BY OUTBACK STEAKHOUSE®
ALICE SPRINGS CHICKEN

INSPIRED BY
CHEESECAKE
FACTORY®

SHRIMP SCAMPI

COPYCAT CHEESECAKE FACTORY SHRIMP SCAMPI

Shrimp scampi is a favorite at restaurants from coast to coast. Give this half-hour copycat a try when you're craving the popular pasta dish but don't want to leave the comforts of home.
—Taste of Home *Test Kitchen*

TAKES: 30 MIN. • **MAKES:** 4 SERVINGS

12   oz. uncooked angel hair pasta
½   cup all-purpose flour
2   Tbsp. grated Parmesan cheese
½   tsp. salt
¼   tsp. pepper
1½   lbs. uncooked shrimp
(26-30 per lb.), peeled and deveined
3   Tbsp. butter

SAUCE
2   Tbsp. olive oil
1   small shallot, chopped
5   garlic cloves
1   cup dry white wine
2   cups heavy whipping cream
2   plum tomatoes, diced
6   fresh basil leaves, thinly sliced
½   tsp. salt
¼   tsp. pepper
2   Tbsp. grated Parmesan cheese

1. Cook pasta according to package directions. Meanwhile, combine flour, Parmesan cheese, salt and pepper in a shallow dish. Add shrimp; turn to coat, shaking off excess flour mixture. In a large skillet, melt butter over medium heat; add shrimp. Cook and stir until the shrimp turn pink, 3-5 minutes. Remove and keep warm.

2. In the same skillet, heat oil over medium heat; add shallot. Cook and stir until tender, about 2-3 minutes. Add garlic cloves; cook 1 minute longer. Stir in wine. Bring to a boil. Reduce heat and simmer, uncovered, until reduced by about half, 3-4 minutes. Stir in cream and simmer, uncovered, until slightly thickened, about 5 minutes. Remove and discard the garlic cloves. Stir in the diced tomatoes, basil, salt, pepper and grated Parmesan cheese.

3. Drain pasta. To serve, spoon sauce into shallow dishes. Top with pasta and shrimp and, if desired, additional basil.

2½ cups: 1121 cal., 64g fat (36g sat. fat), 370mg chol., 993mg sod., 86g carb. (7g sugars, 4g fiber), 46g pro.

COPY THAT!

When preparing this copycat entree, considering using a dry, crisp white wine, such as sauvignon blanc, pinot grigio, an unoaked chardonnay or another high-quality white wine. Select one with a moderate acidity, so it doesn't overwhelm the dish. For a nonalcoholic version, replace the wine with chicken stock and lemon juice. You can also use vegetable or seafood broth with good results.

CHIPOTLE CHICKEN

No need to make a trip to the restaurant chain Chipotle for their famous marinated chicken.
Prepare this easy, flavor-packed grilled chicken at home and get ready for compliments!
The smoky, savory, marinade with a spicy kick and slightly sweet finish is addictive and tastes just
like the restaurant's version! Kids and adults alike love this chicken in bowls, tacos and burritos.

—*Kim Tower, Danville, CA*

PREP: 20 MIN. + MARINATING • **GRILL:** 15 MIN. + STANDING • **MAKES:** 8 SERVINGS

¼ cup water
3 Tbsp. brown sugar
3 Tbsp. white vinegar
3 Tbsp. canola oil
1 Tbsp. chopped chipotle pepper in adobo sauce
5 garlic cloves, halved
1 Tbsp. ground chipotle pepper or ground ancho chile pepper
2½ tsp. ground cumin
2½ tsp. dried oregano
1½ tsp. kosher salt
1 tsp. smoked paprika
½ tsp. pepper
3 lbs. boneless skinless chicken thighs

1. Place the first 12 ingredients in a blender; cover and process until pureed. Transfer marinade to a large bowl or shallow dish. Add the chicken; turn to coat. Refrigerate 8 hours or overnight.

2. Drain chicken, discarding marinade. Grill chicken, covered, over medium-high heat or broil 4 in. from heat until a thermometer reads 170°, 6-8 minutes on each side. Let rest 10 minutes before slicing.

Freeze option: Place cooled chicken in freezer containers. To use, partially thaw in refrigerator overnight. Microwave, covered, on high in a microwave-safe dish until heated through, stirring gently.

4 oz. cooked chicken: 284 cal., 15g fat (4g sat. fat), 113mg chol., 297mg sod., 4g carb. (3g sugars, 0 fiber), 32g pro. **Diabetic exchanges:** 4 lean meat, 2 fat.

INSPIRED BY
CHIPOTLE®
*MARINATED
CHICKEN*

INSPIRED BY
CHEESECAKE FACTORY®
CHICKEN PICCATA

CHEESECAKE FACTORY'S CHICKEN PICCATA

My hungry family rewards me with smiles of satisfaction whenever I serve this meal-in-one dinner.
It's the best payback I can receive, leaving me with the feeling of a job well done at the end of the night!
—*Michelle Stillman, Lancaster, PA*

PREP: 20 MIN. • **COOK:** 30 MIN. • **MAKES:** 4 SERVINGS

12 oz. uncooked angel hair pasta
4 boneless skinless chicken breast halves (6 oz. each)
½ cup all-purpose flour
1¼ tsp. salt, divided
¾ tsp. pepper, divided
2 Tbsp. olive oil, divided
4 Tbsp. butter, divided
¾ lb. sliced fresh mushrooms
1 cup dry white wine or chicken broth
2 Tbsp. lemon juice
½ cup heavy whipping cream
4 tsp. capers, drained
1 Tbsp. minced fresh parsley
Optional: Lemon slices and Parmesan cheese

1. Cook pasta according to the package directions.
2. Flatten chicken to ¼-in. thickness. In a shallow bowl, mix flour, ¾ tsp. salt and ½ tsp. pepper. Dip chicken in flour mixture to coat both sides; shake off excess.
3. In a large skillet, heat 1 Tbsp. oil and 2 Tbsp. butter over medium heat; add chicken. Cook until chicken juices run clear, about 3-5 minutes on each side. Remove and keep warm.
4. In same pan, heat remaining 1 Tbsp. oil and 2 Tbsp. butter over medium heat; add the mushrooms. Cook and stir until tender, 5-7 minutes. Add wine and lemon juice, stirring to loosen browned bits from pan. Bring to a boil; cook until liquid is reduced by about half, roughly 5-7 minutes. Reduce heat to low. Stir in the cream, capers and remaining ½ tsp. salt and ¼ tsp. pepper; heat through.
5. Drain pasta. Serve chicken with the pasta and sauce. Sprinkle with parsley and, if desired, serve with lemon and Parmesan cheese.

1 chicken breast with ½ cup sauce and 1½ cups pasta:
865 cal., 35g fat (17g sat. fat), 158mg chol., 998mg sod., 81g carb. (5g sugars, 4g fiber), 51g pro.

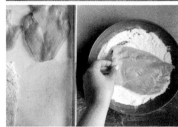

PICCATA-MAKING POINTERS

- Cover the chicken breasts with plastic wrap before flattening for easy cleanup.
- Set floured chicken on a nearby sheet pan.
- Move the chicken only to flip it in the pan. This creates a golden crust on the outside of the chicken.

KUNG PAO CHICKEN

My family loves the kung pao chicken from our favorite Chinese restaurant. But in less time than it takes for the delivery guy to arrive, we can be digging into a steaming platter of this copycat recipe.
—*Jennifer Beckman, Falls Church, VA*

PREP: 25 MIN. • **COOK:** 15 MIN. • **MAKES:** 4 SERVINGS

1 lb. boneless skinless chicken breasts, cut into ¾-in. cubes
3 tsp. cornstarch, divided
½ tsp. salt
½ tsp. pepper
2 Tbsp. chicken stock
2 Tbsp. hoisin sauce
1 Tbsp. reduced-sodium soy sauce
1 Tbsp. oyster sauce
½ tsp. Sriracha chili sauce or ¼ tsp. hot pepper sauce
2 Tbsp. peanut oil, divided
1 small red onion, chopped
1 medium sweet red pepper, chopped
2 garlic cloves, minced
1 tsp. minced fresh gingerroot
¼ cup minced fresh cilantro
¼ cup dry roasted peanuts

1. In a large bowl, combine the chicken, 1 tsp. cornstarch, salt and pepper; set aside.

2. Place remaining 2 tsp. cornstarch in a small bowl. Stir in the stock, hoisin sauce, soy sauce, oyster sauce and chili sauce until smooth.

3. In a large skillet or wok, stir-fry chicken in batches in 1 Tbsp. oil until no longer pink. Remove and keep warm.

4. Stir-fry onion and red pepper in the remaining 1 Tbsp. oil until vegetables are crisp-tender, 2-5 minutes. Add garlic and ginger and cook 1 minute longer.

5. Stir cornstarch mixture and add to the pan. Bring to a boil; cook and stir for 2 minutes or until thickened. Add chicken; heat through. Stir in cilantro and peanuts.

¾ cup: 285 cal., 14g fat (3g sat. fat), 63mg chol., 857mg sod., 13g carb. (5g sugars, 2g fiber), 26g pro.

INSPIRED BY
PANDA EXPRESS®
KUNG PAO CHICKEN

BROILED LOBSTER TAILS

No matter where you live, these succulent, buttery lobster tails are just a few minutes away. Here in Iowa, we use frozen lobster with delicious results, but if you're near the ocean, by all means use fresh!

—*Lauren McAnelly, Des Moines, IA*

PREP: 30 MIN. • **COOK:** 5 MIN. • **MAKES:** 4 SERVINGS

4 lobster tails (5 to 6 oz. each), thawed
¼ cup cold butter, cut into thin slices
Salt and pepper to taste
Lemon wedges

COPY THAT!

This recipe may be prepared using a compound herb butter in place of plain butter. See recipes at right.

1. Preheat broiler. Using kitchen scissors, cut a 2-in.-wide rectangle from the top shell of each lobster tail; loosen from the lobster meat and remove.

2. Pull away edges of remaining shell to release the lobster meat from the sides; pry meat loose from bottom shell, keeping tail end attached. Place in a foil-lined 15x10x1-in. pan. Arrange butter slices over lobster meat.

3. Broil 5-6 in. from heat until meat is opaque, 5-8 minutes. Season with salt and pepper to taste; serve with lemon wedges.

1 lobster tail: 211 cal., 13g fat (8g sat. fat), 211mg chol., 691mg sod., 0 carb. (0 sugars, 0 fiber), 24g pro.

Compound Butter: Process ¼ cup softened butter with fresh herbs and seasonings of choice in a small food processor. Transfer mixture to a sheet of waxed paper; roll into a log, then refrigerate until firm. To use, unwrap and cut into thin slices.

Lemon-Chive Compound Butter: Add 2 Tbsp. chopped fresh chives, 2 Tbsp. chopped fresh parsley, 1 Tbsp. minced shallot, 1 minced garlic clove, ½ tsp. grated lemon peel and ¼ tsp. salt to butter.

Chimichurri Compound Butter: Add 2 Tbsp. chopped fresh cilantro, 2 Tbsp. chopped fresh parsley, 1 Tbsp. minced shallot, 1 tsp. grated lemon peel, 1 tsp. minced fresh oregano, 1 minced garlic clove, ¼ tsp. salt and ⅛ tsp. crushed red pepper flakes to butter.

EASY HONEY MUSTARD CHICKEN

My absolute favorite dish at Bakers Square is the Honey Mustard Chicken with mushrooms and onions. Unfortunately, the Bakers Square restaurants near me relocated, so I devised my own. Best of all, it's quick and easy.
—*Arlene Erlbach, Morton Grove, IL*

PREP: 15 MIN. • **COOK:** 25 MIN. • **MAKES:** 4 SERVINGS

¾ cup Dijon honey mustard salad dressing
⅓ cup chicken broth
⅓ cup half-and-half cream
¼ tsp. salt
¼ tsp. pepper
¼ cup all-purpose flour
4 boneless skinless chicken breast halves (6 oz. each)
3 Tbsp. olive oil, divided
½ lb. medium fresh mushrooms, thinly sliced
1 large sweet onion, halved and thinly sliced

1. In a small bowl, combine the first 5 ingredients. Place flour in a shallow bowl. Add chicken, a few pieces at a time, and toss to coat; shake off excess. In a large skillet, heat 2 Tbsp. oil over medium-high heat. Brown chicken on both sides. Remove from pan. Add mushrooms and onion to same pan; cook and stir until tender, 6-8 minutes.

2. Add dressing mixture, stirring to loosen browned bits from pan. Return chicken to pan; bring to a boil. Reduce the heat and simmer, uncovered, until a thermometer inserted in chicken reads 165°, 12-15 minutes longer.

1 serving: 563 cal., 35g fat (6g sat. fat), 117mg chol., 548mg sod., 23g carb. (12g sugars, 1g fiber), 38g pro.

INSPIRED BY
BAKERS SQUARE®
HONEY MUSTARD CHICKEN

INSPIRED BY
THE HONEY BAKED
HAM COMPANY®
HONEY BAKED HAM

HONEY BAKED HAM

For holidays and special occasions my family loves a good old-fashioned baked ham. One year I decided to see if I could duplicate the crunchy glaze we enjoy so much. After a few tries, I created a great copycat. Now, I'm asked to bring the ham to all sorts of potlucks and parties. The best part is how easy it is!
—*Donna Gribbins, Shelbyville, KY*

PREP: 10 MIN. • **COOK:** 4 HOURS 5 MIN. + STANDING • **MAKES:** 16 SERVINGS

1 spiral-sliced fully cooked
  bone-in ham (8 to 10 lbs.)
1 cup water
¾ cup honey, divided

GLAZE
1 cup sugar
½ tsp. ground cinnamon
½ tsp. ground allspice
½ tsp. pepper
½ tsp. paprika
¼ tsp. ground ginger
¼ tsp. ground nutmeg
¼ tsp. ground mustard
¼ tsp. Chinese five-spice powder
⅛ tsp. ground cloves

1. Place ham and water in a 7-qt. slow cooker. Brush ham with ½ cup honey. Cook, covered, on low until a thermometer reads 140°, 4 to 5 hours.

2. Preheat broiler. Combine glaze ingredients. Transfer ham to a rack in a shallow roasting pan, cut side down. Brush with remaining ¼ cup honey; sprinkle with glaze mixture, carefully pressing to adhere. Broil 6-8 in. from heat until lightly browned and the sugar is melted, about 3-5 minutes, rotating as needed. Cover with foil; let stand until the glaze hardens, about 30 minutes.

5 oz. cooked ham: 288 cal., 6g fat (2g sat. fat), 100mg chol., 1192mg sod., 26g carb. (26g sugars, 0 fiber), 33g pro.

COPYCAT CAFE RIO SWEET PORK

My friends are big fans of Cafe Rio's sweet pork tacos, so I came up with this fake-out to eat in the comfort of our own homes. Serve the pork in flour tortillas or taco shells, or enjoy it in these meal-in-one bowls.

—Donna Gribbins, Shelbyville, KY

PREP: 20 MIN. + MARINATING • **COOK:** 10 HOURS • **MAKES:** 8 SERVINGS

2   cans (12 oz. each) cola, divided
1   cup packed brown sugar, divided
1   bone-in pork shoulder roast (5 to 7 lbs.)
1   Tbsp. kosher salt
1   Tbsp. garlic powder
1   Tbsp. onion powder
1   tsp. pepper
1½ cups enchilada sauce
1   can (7 oz.) chopped green chiles
    Hot cooked rice, optional
    Optional toppings: Black beans, chopped red onion, crumbled Cotija cheese and salsa

1. In a large bowl or shallow dish, combine 1 can cola and ½ cup brown sugar. Add pork; turn to coat. Cover and refrigerate 8 hours or overnight.
2. Drain pork, discarding marinade. Place pork in a 5- or 6-qt. slow cooker. Add salt, garlic powder, onion powder, pepper and remaining can of cola. Cook, covered, on low until meat is tender, 8-10 hours.
3. Set meat aside until cool enough to handle. Remove meat from bones; discard bones. Shred meat with 2 forks. Discard cooking juices and return meat to slow cooker. Stir in enchilada sauce, green chiles and remaining ½ cup brown sugar. Cook, covered, on low until heated through, about 2 hours.
4. Serve pork in bowls over rice with toppings as desired.

Freeze option: Freeze cooled meat mixture in freezer containers. To use, partially thaw in refrigerator overnight. Heat through in a saucepan, stirring occasionally.

1 cup cooked pork: 419 cal., 22g fat (8g sat. fat), 125mg chol., 560mg sod., 18g carb. (15g sugars, 0 fiber), 37g pro.

INSPIRED BY
CAFE RIO®
SWEET PORK

INSPIRED BY
CRACKER
BARREL®
MEAT LOAF

COPYCAT CRACKER BARREL MEAT LOAF

If you've never been a fan of meat loaf, we're pretty sure this version is about to change your mind. While some homemade meat loaves tend to be dry and not-so-tasty, this copycat entree is packed with flavor and melt-in-your-mouth goodness.

—Taste of Home *Test Kitchen*

PREP: 15 MIN. • **BAKE:** 1 HOUR + STANDING • **MAKES:** 12 SERVINGS

2 large eggs, beaten
⅓ cup 2% milk
1½ cups shredded cheddar cheese
1 sleeve crushed Ritz crackers (30 crackers)
½ cup finely chopped onion
½ cup finely chopped green pepper
½ tsp. salt
¼ tsp. garlic powder
¼ tsp. pepper
2 lbs. ground beef
½ cup ketchup
3 Tbsp. brown sugar
2 tsp. Dijon or yellow mustard

1. Preheat oven to 350°. In a large bowl, combine eggs, milk, cheese, crackers, onion, green pepper, salt, garlic powder and pepper. Crumble beef over mixture and mix lightly but thoroughly. Shape into a 5x10-in. loaf in an ungreased 13x9-in. baking dish. Bake, uncovered, for 50 minutes.
2. Meanwhile, in a small bowl, combine ketchup, brown sugar and mustard. Spoon over the meat loaf.
3. Bake until a thermometer reads 160°, 10-15 minutes longer. Let loaf stand for 10 minutes before slicing.

1 piece: 305 cal., 19g fat (8g sat. fat), 99mg chol., 504mg sod., 13g carb. (7g sugars, 0 fiber), 20g pro.

TRADE SECRETS

- Combine the ingredients with a spatula to help prevent over mixing.
- Cook uncovered for a crispier exterior and a juicy interior,
- Both Dijon and yellow mustard work in the sauce, so feel free to use what you have on hand.
- Be generous with the sauce. Brush on an even layer over the top and sides.

GARLIC-LEMON SHRIMP LINGUINE

The Cheesecake Factory has an extensive menu, but I always seem to order their delicious fresh and citrusy Lemon Shrimp Linguine. I'd enjoyed it enough times that I was confident I could reproduce it to share with friends and family. I think I hit it spot on! When I have fresh basil from the garden, I use that instead of parsley.

—*Trisha Kruse, Eagle, ID*

TAKES: 30 MIN. • **MAKES:** 4 SERVINGS

8 oz. uncooked linguine
2 Tbsp. olive oil
1 Tbsp. butter
1 lb. uncooked shrimp (26-30 per lb.), peeled and deveined
3 garlic cloves, minced
1 Tbsp. grated lemon zest
1 Tbsp. lemon juice
1 tsp. lemon-pepper seasoning
2 Tbsp. minced fresh parsley

1. Cook linguine according to package directions for al dente. Meanwhile, in a large skillet, heat oil and butter over medium-high heat. Add shrimp; cook and stir 3 minutes. Add garlic, lemon zest, juice and lemon pepper; cook and stir until the shrimp turn pink, 2-3 minutes longer. Stir in parsley.

2. Drain the linguine, reserving ⅓ cup pasta water. Add enough reserved pasta water to shrimp mixture to achieve desired consistency. Serve with linguine.

1 serving: 387 cal., 12g fat (3g sat. fat), 146mg chol., 239mg sod., 43g carb. (2g sugars, 2g fiber), 26g pro.

WHY YOU'LL LOVE IT...

"This is so easy to make! The garlic-lemon sauce is fresh and bright, which is a nice change from heavy pasta sauces. This is a brand-new favorite for my weeknight dinner rotation."
—SUSAN8352, TASTEOFHOME.COM

INSPIRED BY
CHEESECAKE FACTORY®
LEMON SHRIMP LINGUINE

**INSPIRED BY
THE CHEESECAKE
FACTORY®**

*SPICY CASHEW
CHICKEN*

CASHEW CHICKEN WITH GINGER

There are lots of recipes for cashew chicken, but my family thinks this one stands alone.
We love the flavor from the fresh ginger and the crunch of the cashews. Plus, it's easy to prepare.

—Oma Rollison, El Cajon, CA

TAKES: 30 MIN. • **MAKES:** 6 SERVINGS

2 Tbsp. cornstarch
1 Tbsp. brown sugar
1¼ cups chicken broth
2 Tbsp. soy sauce
3 Tbsp. canola oil, divided
1½ lbs. boneless skinless chicken breasts, cut into 1-in. pieces
½ lb. sliced fresh mushrooms
1 small green pepper, cut into strips
1 can (8 oz.) sliced water chestnuts, drained
1½ tsp. grated fresh gingerroot
4 green onions, sliced
¾ cup salted cashews
Hot cooked rice

1. Mix first 4 ingredients until smooth. In a large skillet, heat 2 Tbsp. oil over medium-high heat; stir-fry chicken until no longer pink. Remove from pan.

2. In same pan, heat remaining 1 Tbsp. oil over medium-high heat; stir-fry mushrooms, pepper, water chestnuts and ginger until pepper is crisp-tender, 3-5 minutes. Stir broth mixture and add to pan with green onions; bring to a boil. Cook and stir until sauce is thickened, 1-2 minutes.

3. Stir in chicken and cashews; heat through. Serve with rice.

¾ cup chicken mixture: 349 cal., 19g fat (3g sat. fat), 64mg chol., 650mg sod., 18g carb. (6g sugars, 2g fiber), 28g pro. **Diabetic exchanges:** 3 lean meat, 3 fat, 1 starch.

INSPIRED BY
OLIVE GARDEN®
FRIED LASAGNA

POPULAR PIZZA & PASTA

Mangia! Turn your kitchen into an Italian eatery when you whip up any of the following dishes at home. Surprise the gang with a hearty, cheesy favorite tonight.

PRETZEL CRUST PIZZA

In our house, we love pizza and pretzel bread! When Little Caesar's came out with its pretzel crust pizza, we fell in love but also knew it was unrealistic to be buying it all the time. The next best thing was to make it ourselves, and it came out even better than we hoped. This thick-crusted copycat pizza is bound to blow your socks off!

—*Mary Lou Timpson, Centennial Park, AZ*

PREP: 25 IN. + RISING • **BAKE:** 20 MIN. • **MAKES:** 8 SERVINGS

- 1½ cups warm water (110° to 115°)
- 2 Tbsp. sugar
- 1 Tbsp. active dry yeast
- 4 cups all-purpose flour
- 1 tsp. salt
- ½ cup hot water
- 2 Tbsp. baking soda
- ¼ tsp. pretzel or coarse salt

PIZZA
- ½ cup prepared salsa con queso dip
- 2 cups shredded Mexican cheese blend
- ½ cup sliced pepperoni
- 1 Tbsp. butter, melted

1. In a stand mixer, stir together warm water, sugar and yeast; let stand until foamy, 4-5 minutes. Add flour and 1 tsp. table salt. Using a dough hook, mix on low speed until the dough comes together, 1-2 minutes. Increase speed to medium and mix for an additional 5 minutes. Place in a greased bowl, turning once to grease the top. Cover and let rise in a warm place until doubled, about 45 minutes.

2. Preheat oven to 425°. Punch down dough; press into a 12-in. circle onto an ungreased 14-in. pizza pan. Let stand 10 minutes. Stir together hot water and baking soda; brush mixture over outer 1-in. Let stand 5 minutes; repeat. Sprinkle coarse salt over the edge.

3. Spread queso dip over inside of crust. Top with cheese and pepperoni. Bake until crust is golden brown and cheese is melted, 16-18 minutes. Brush the crust with melted butter before serving.

1 piece: 414 cal., 15g fat (7g sat. fat), 36mg chol., 772mg sod., 55g carb. (4g sugars, 3g fiber), 15g pro.

HAVE IT YOUR WAY.

This pizza recipe is delicious no matter how you top it, but the cheese sauce really does make it just like Little Caesar's version. However, if you'd like to use your own homemade pizza sauce or your favorite store-bought sauce, go ahead and enjoy!

INSPIRED BY
LITTLE CAESAR'S®
PRETZEL CRUST

**INSPIRED BY
CHEESECAKE FACTORY®**
PASTA DI VINCI

COPYCAT PASTA DA VINCI

I fell in love with this dish at the restaurant and experimented until I could duplicate it. I think mine is just as good, if not better! The sauce can be made ahead and refrigerated or frozen. Thaw if frozen and warm gently in a large skillet. Cook pasta and you have a delicious dinner on a weeknight.

—Trisha Kruse, Eagle, ID

PREP: 25 MIN. • **COOK:** 35 MIN. • **MAKES:** 8 SERVINGS

1 pkg. (16 oz.) penne pasta
1 large red onion, diced
2 Tbsp. olive oil
3 garlic cloves, minced
1½ lbs. boneless skinless chicken breasts, cubed
½ lb. sliced fresh mushrooms
2 cups dry white wine
1 can (14½ oz.) beef broth
1 pkg. (8 oz.) cream cheese, softened
½ cup butter, softened
½ cup half-and-half cream, room temperature
½ tsp. salt
¼ tsp. pepper
½ cup grated Parmesan cheese, divided
   Minced fresh parsley, optional

1. Cook pasta according to package directions for al dente. Meanwhile, in a large skillet, cook onion in oil over medium heat until softened, 4-5 minutes. Add garlic and cook 1 minute longer. Stir in chicken and mushrooms. Cook, stirring frequently, until chicken is no longer pink, about 5-7 minutes. With a slotted spoon, remove chicken-onion mixture; set aside.

2. To the same skillet, add wine and broth; bring mixture to a simmer. Cook until the liquid is reduced by half, 15-20 minutes. Reduce heat to low; add cream cheese and butter, whisking until melted. Whisk in cream, salt and pepper. Add chicken mixture to pan; heat through on low. Toss with pasta and ¼ cup Parmesan cheese. Top with the remaining ¼ cup Parmesan cheese and, if desired, parsley.

1½ cups: 634 cal., 31g fat (16g sat. fat), 118mg chol., 706mg sod., 49g carb. (5g sugars, 3g fiber), 30g pro.

COPY THAT!

If you don't have white wine on hand, such as pinot grigio or chardonnay, you can substitute something different. For instance, full-flavored Madeira wine is a great option, as is Marsala wine or any other semisweet wine. Note that swapping out the white wine with another option could greatly change the overall flavor of the final dish.

FIVE-CHEESE ZITI AL FORNO

After having the five-cheese ziti at Olive Garden, I tried to make my own homemade version—and I think I got pretty close. I always double this and freeze the second one for another meal.

—Keri Whitney, Castro Valley, CA

PREP: 20 MIN. • **BAKE:** 30 MIN. + STANDING • **MAKES:** 12 SERVINGS

1½ lbs. (about 7½ cups) uncooked ziti or small tube pasta
2 jars (24 oz. each) marinara sauce
1 jar (15 oz.) Alfredo sauce
2 cups shredded part-skim mozzarella cheese, divided
½ cup reduced-fat ricotta cheese
½ cup shredded provolone cheese
½ cup grated Romano cheese

TOPPING
½ cup grated Parmesan cheese
½ cup panko bread crumbs
3 garlic cloves, minced
2 Tbsp. olive oil
Optional: Minced fresh parsley or basil, optional

1. Preheat oven to 350°. Cook the pasta according to the package directions for al dente; drain.
2. Meanwhile, in a large Dutch oven, combine the marinara sauce, Alfredo sauce, 1 cup mozzarella and the ricotta, provolone and Romano. Cook over medium heat until sauce begins to simmer and cheeses are melted. Stir in cooked pasta; pour mixture into a greased 13x9-in. baking dish. Top with remaining 1 cup mozzarella cheese.
3. In a small bowl, stir together Parmesan, bread crumbs, garlic and olive oil; sprinkle over the pasta.
4. Bake, uncovered, until mixture is bubbly and topping is golden brown, 30-40 minutes. Let stand 10 minutes before serving. Garnish with fresh parsley or basil if desired.

Freeze option: Cool the unbaked casserole; cover and freeze. To use, partially thaw in the refrigerator overnight. Remove from refrigerator 30 minutes before baking. Preheat oven to 350°. Cover casserole with foil; bake 50 minutes. Uncover; bake until heated through and a thermometer inserted in center reads 165°, 15-20 minutes longer.

1 cup: 449 cal., 15g fat (8g sat. fat), 32mg chol., 960mg sod., 59g carb. (11g sugars, 4g fiber), 21g pro.

INSPIRED BY
OLIVE
GARDEN®

FIVE-CHEESE
ZITI AL FORNO

INSPIRED BY
ROMANO'S MACARONI GRILL®
CHICKEN MARSALA

SPEEDY CHICKEN MARSALA

Because this is one of our favorite dishes to order in restaurants, I created
my own version that could be made in a flash for weeknight dinners.

—Trisha Kruse, Eagle, ID

TAKES: 30 MIN. • **MAKES:** 4 SERVINGS

8 oz. uncooked whole wheat or
   multigrain angel hair pasta
4 boneless skinless chicken
   breast halves (5 oz. each)
¼ cup all-purpose flour
1 tsp. lemon-pepper seasoning
½ tsp. salt
2 Tbsp. olive oil, divided
4 cups sliced fresh mushrooms
1 garlic clove, minced
1 cup dry Marsala wine

WHY YOU'LL LOVE IT...

"My family loves this dish. My daughter said she can't order this when dining out anymore, as those entrees cannot compare with this version."
—LESLIE KERNOZEK, TASTEOFHOME.COM

1. Cook pasta according to package directions. Pound chicken with a meat mallet to ¼-in. thickness. In a large resealable bag or container, mix the flour, lemon pepper and salt. Add chicken, 1 piece at a time; close bag or container and shake to coat.

2. In a large skillet, heat 1 Tbsp. oil over medium heat. Add chicken; cook for 4-5 minutes on each side or until no longer pink. Remove from pan.

3. In the same skillet, heat remaining 1 Tbsp. oil over medium-high heat. Add mushrooms; cook and stir until tender. Add garlic and cook 1 minute longer. Add wine; bring to a boil. Cook for 5-6 minutes or until liquid is reduced by half, stirring to loosen browned bits from pan. Return chicken to pan, turning to coat with sauce; heat through.

4. Drain pasta; serve with chicken mixture.

1 serving: 493 cal., 11g fat (2g sat. fat), 78mg chol., 279mg sod., 50g carb. (4g sugars, 7g fiber), 40g pro.

BLUSHING PENNE PASTA

I reworked this recipe from an original that called for vodka and heavy whipping cream.
My friends and family had a hard time believing a sauce this rich, flavorful and creamy could be light.

—Margaret Wilson, San Bernardino, CA

TAKES: 30 MIN. • **MAKES:** 8 SERVINGS

1 pkg. (16 oz.) penne pasta
2 Tbsp. butter
1 medium onion, halved and thinly sliced
2 Tbsp. minced fresh thyme or 2 tsp. dried thyme
2 Tbsp. minced fresh basil or 2 tsp. dried basil
1 tsp. salt
1½ cups half-and-half cream, divided
½ cup white wine or reduced-sodium chicken broth
1 Tbsp. tomato paste
2 Tbsp. all-purpose flour
½ cup shredded Parmigiano-Reggiano cheese, divided

1. In a 6-qt. stockpot, cook pasta according to package directions. Drain; return to pot.

2. Meanwhile, in a large nonstick skillet, heat butter over medium heat; saute onion until lightly browned, 8-10 minutes. Add herbs and salt; cook and stir 1 minute. Add 1 cup cream, wine and tomato paste; cook and stir until blended.

3. Mix flour and remaining ½ cup cream until smooth; gradually stir into onion mixture. Bring to a boil; cook and stir until thickened, about 2 minutes. Stir in ¼ cup cheese. Stir into the pasta. Serve with remaining ¼ cup cheese.

1 cup: 335 cal., 10g fat (6g sat. fat), 34mg chol., 431mg sod., 47g carb. (4g sugars, 2g fiber), 12g pro.

INSPIRED BY
NOODLES &
COMPANY®
PENNE ROSA

INSPIRED BY
OLIVE GARDEN®

*ASIAGO TORTELLONI ALFREDO
WITH GRILLED CHICKEN*

ASIAGO TORTELLINI ALFREDO WITH GRILLED CHICKEN

My family loves all types of pasta and this is one of their favorite dishes.
Swap out the flavor of tortelloni or tortellini if you can't find any with Asiago.

—Susan Hein, Burlington, WI

TAKES: 30 MIN. • **MAKES:** 4 SERVINGS

4   boneless skinless chicken
    breasts (6 oz. each)
1   Tbsp. olive oil
½   tsp. salt
¼   tsp. pepper
1   pkg. (9 oz.) refrigerated cheese
    tortellini
1   jar (15 oz.) Alfredo sauce,
    warmed
½   cup grated Asiago cheese

1. Pound chicken breasts with a meat mallet to ½-in. thickness. Brush with oil and sprinkle with salt and pepper. Place chicken on oiled grill rack. Grill, covered, over medium heat until a thermometer reads 165°, about 4-5 minutes on each side.

2. Meanwhile, cook tortellini according to package directions. Preheat broiler. Drain tortellini and toss with hot Alfredo sauce. Transfer to a greased broiler-safe 9-in. square baking dish; sprinkle with Asiago. Broil 3-4 in. from heat until top is golden brown, 2-3 minutes.

3. To serve, slice chicken and place on top of tortellini. Sprinkle with additional Asiago if desired.

1 chicken breast half with 1 cup pasta: 543 cal., 24g fat (12g sat. fat), 153mg chol., 1161mg sod., 31g carb. (1g sugars, 2g fiber), 48g pro.

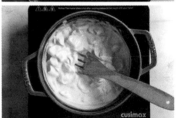

TEST KITCHEN TIPS
• A silicone brush works best for brushing on the oil.
• Don't feel like grilling? Broil the chicken in the oven or the stovetop in a skillet.
• If you don't like jarred Alfredo sauce, feel free to use your own Alfredo recipe.
• We sprinkled on more Asiago before broiling, but you can add Parmesan or a cheese blend.

CALIFORNIA CHICKEN CLUB PIZZA

Inspired by the California Club pizza from California Pizza Kitchen, I decided to whip up my own version.
It's loaded with veggies, cheese, bacon, chicken and even avocado.

—Robert Pickart, Chicago, IL

PREP: 25 MIN. • **BAKE:** 10 MIN. • **MAKES:** 4 SERVINGS

1   Tbsp. cornmeal
1   loaf (1 lb.) frozen pizza dough, thawed
1   cup shredded mozzarella cheese
1   cup ready-to-use grilled chicken breast strips
4   bacon strips, cooked and crumbled
2   cups shredded romaine
1   cup fresh arugula
¼   cup mayonnaise
1   Tbsp. lemon juice
1   tsp. grated lemon zest
½   tsp. pepper
1   medium tomato, thinly sliced
1   medium ripe avocado, peeled and sliced
¼   cup loosely packed basil leaves, chopped

1. Preheat oven to 450°. Grease a 14-in. pizza pan; sprinkle with cornmeal. On a floured surface, roll dough into a 13-in. circle. Transfer to prepared pan; build up edges slightly. Sprinkle with cheese, chicken and bacon. Bake until crust is lightly browned, 10-12 minutes.

2. Meanwhile, place romaine and arugula in a large bowl. In a small bowl, combine mayonnaise, lemon juice, lemon zest and pepper. Pour over lettuces; toss to coat. Arrange over warm pizza. Top with tomato, avocado and basil. Serve immediately.

Note: We used Rhodes Bake N Serv Pizza Dough to test this recipe.

2 slices: 612 cal., 30g fat (7g sat. fat), 51mg chol., 859mg sod., 59g carb. (4g sugars, 5g fiber), 29g pro.

INSPIRED BY
CALIFORNIA
PIZZA KITCHEN

*CALIFORNIA CLUB
PIZZA*

INSPIRED BY
OLIVE GARDEN®
MEAT SAUCE

PASTA NAPOLITANA

This is the ultimate meat lovers pasta and is my copycat version of an Olive Garden dish. Rich and hearty, with tremendous flavors, this pasta always disappears quickly. I like to make extra sauce, as it freezes well.
—*John Pittman, Northampton, PA*

PREP: 30 MIN. • **COOK:** 2 HOURS • **MAKES:** 8 SERVINGS

8 bacon strips
1 lb. ground beef
1 lb. bulk Italian sausage
1 Tbsp. olive oil
1 large onion, chopped
1 can (6 oz.) tomato paste
1 jar (24 oz.) marinara sauce
1 can (14½ oz.) chicken broth
½ cup dry red wine
1 can (8 oz.) mushroom stems
   and pieces
⅓ cup pepperoni, chopped
1 Tbsp. sugar
1 Tbsp. garlic powder
1 Tbsp. dried oregano
1 Tbsp. dried basil
2 tsp. dried parsley flakes
1 tsp. dried rosemary, crushed
1 tsp. dried marjoram
1 tsp. rubbed sage
1 tsp. seasoned salt
1 tsp. pepper
½ to 1 tsp. crushed red pepper
   flakes
1 tsp. Worcestershire sauce
   Hot cooked spaghetti
   Grated Parmesan cheese

1. In a Dutch oven, cook bacon over medium heat; drain and set aside. Discard drippings. In same pan, cook ground beef and sausage in olive oil until beef is no longer pink, breaking meat into crumbles. Add onion; cook until tender, about 5 minutes. Drain. Add tomato paste; cook and stir until fragrant, about 5 minutes. Stir in bacon, marinara sauce, broth, wine, mushrooms, pepperoni, sugar, garlic powder, oregano, basil, parsley, rosemary, marjoram, sage, seasoned salt, pepper, pepper flakes and Worcestershire sauce.
2. Bring to a boil; reduce heat. Simmer, covered, stirring occasionally, until thickened and flavors have combined, about 2 hours. Serve with spaghetti and Parmesan cheese.

1 serving: 427 cal., 28g fat (9g sat. fat), 82mg chol., 1591mg sod., 19g carb. (10g sugars, 4g fiber), 24g pro.

CAJUN CHICKEN & PASTA

This kicked-up pasta dish is a family favorite and my most requested recipe. It's easy to adapt, too. Substitute shrimp for the chicken, add your favorite veggies and adjust the spice level to your family's taste. You can't go wrong!

—Dolly Kragel, Sloan, IA

PREP: 10 MIN. + STANDING • **COOK:** 35 MIN. • **MAKES:** 6 SERVINGS

1 lb. boneless skinless chicken breasts, cut into 2x½-in. strips
3 tsp. Cajun seasoning
8 oz. uncooked penne pasta (about 2⅓ cups)
2 Tbsp. butter, divided
1 small sweet red pepper, diced
1 small green pepper, diced
½ cup sliced fresh mushrooms
4 green onions, chopped
1 cup heavy whipping cream
½ tsp. salt
¼ tsp. dried basil
¼ tsp. lemon-pepper seasoning
¼ tsp. garlic powder
  Pepper to taste
  Chopped plum tomatoes
  Minced fresh basil
  Shredded Parmesan cheese

1. Toss chicken with Cajun seasoning; let stand 15 minutes. Cook pasta according to package directions; drain.

2. In a large skillet, heat 1 Tbsp. butter over medium-high heat; saute chicken until no longer pink, 5-6 minutes. Remove from the pan.

3. In same pan, heat remaining 1 Tbsp. butter over medium-high heat; saute peppers, mushrooms and green onions until peppers are crisp-tender, 6-8 minutes. Stir in cream and seasonings; bring to a boil. Cook and stir until slightly thickened, 4-6 minutes. Stir in pasta and chicken; heat through. Top with tomatoes and basil. Sprinkle with cheese.

1 serving: 398 cal., 21g fat (12g sat. fat), 97mg chol., 357mg sod., 31g carb. (4g sugars, 2g fiber), 22g pro.

COPY THAT!

There are several different Cajun spice blends on the market today. They all contain peppers (black pepper, cayenne and possibly others), garlic and paprika. You can make your own basic blend and then add different spices to suit your preference if you'd like.

INSPIRED BY
CHILI'S®

*CAJUN
CHICKEN
PASTA*

INSPIRED BY
SBARRO®

*PEPPERONI
STROMBOLI*

ITALIAN MEAT STROMBOLI

As a mother of two, I seem to have time for creativity only when I'm in the kitchen. I love the Pepperoni Stromboli from Sbarro's but didn't have enough pepperoni, so I added a little ham as well.
—*Denise Tutton, Ridgway, PA*

PREP: 25 MIN. + RISING • **BAKE:** 25 MIN. • **MAKES:** 10 SERVINGS

1 loaf (1 lb.) frozen bread dough, thawed
1 can (8 oz.) pizza sauce
¼ tsp. garlic powder, divided
¼ tsp. dried oregano, divided
8 oz. brick cheese, sliced
1 cup shredded part-skim mozzarella cheese
½ cup chopped green pepper
¼ cup chopped onion
1 cup sliced fresh mushrooms
½ cup shredded Parmesan cheese
1 pkg. (3 oz.) sliced pepperoni
5 oz. sliced deli ham

1. Place dough in a greased bowl, turning once to grease the top. Cover and let rise in a warm place until doubled, about 1 hour.
2. Preheat oven to 350°. Mix pizza sauce and ⅛ tsp. each garlic powder and oregano.
3. Punch down dough. On a lightly floured surface, roll dough into a 15x10-in. rectangle. Top with brick cheese, sauce mixture and remaining ingredients to within 1 in. of edges.
4. Roll up, jelly-roll style, starting with a long side. Pinch seam to seal and tuck the ends under; transfer to a greased baking sheet. Sprinkle with remaining ⅛ tsp. each garlic powder and oregano. Bake until golden brown, 25-30 minutes.

1 piece: 335 cal., 16g fat (8g sat. fat), 46mg chol., 871mg sod., 27g carb. (4g sugars, 3g fiber), 19g pro.

HOMEMADE MEATLESS SPAGHETTI SAUCE

When my tomatoes ripen, the first things I make are BLTs and this homemade spaghetti sauce.
—*Sondra Bergy, Lowell, MI*

PREP: 20 MIN. • **COOK:** 3¼ HOURS • **MAKES:** 2 QT.

4   medium onions, chopped
½   cup canola oil
12 cups chopped peeled fresh
    tomatoes
4   garlic cloves, minced
3   bay leaves
4   tsp. salt
2   tsp. dried oregano
1¼ tsp. pepper
½   tsp. dried basil
2   cans (6 oz. each) tomato paste
⅓   cup packed brown sugar
    Hot cooked pasta
    Minced fresh basil, optional

1. In a Dutch oven, saute the onions in oil until tender. Add the tomatoes, garlic, bay leaves, salt, oregano, pepper and basil. Bring to a boil. Reduce heat; cover and simmer for 2 hours, stirring the sauce occasionally.

2. Add tomato paste and brown sugar; simmer, uncovered, for 1 hour. Discard bay leaves. Serve with pasta and, if desired, basil. **½ cup:** 133 cal., 7g fat (1g sat. fat), 0 chol., 614mg sod., 17g carb. (12g sugars, 3g fiber), 2g pro.

COPY THAT!
Browned ground beef or Italian sausage can be added to the cooked sauce if desired. The sauce also freezes well.

HOMEMADE FETTUCCINE ALFREDO

This easy Alfredo sauce is creamy and comforting, and it coats fettuccine noodles in fine fashion. It tastes surprisingly close to the Olive Garden's Alfredo, if you ask me.
—*Jo Gray, Park City, MT*

TAKES: 20 MIN. • **MAKES:** 2 SERVINGS

4   oz. uncooked fettuccine
3   Tbsp. butter
1   cup heavy whipping cream
¼   cup plus 2 Tbsp. grated
    Parmesan cheese, divided
¼   cup grated Romano cheese
1   large egg yolk, lightly beaten
⅛   tsp. salt
    Dash each pepper and ground
    nutmeg
    Minced fresh parsley, optional

Cook fettuccine according to package directions. Meanwhile, in a saucepan, melt butter over medium-low heat. Stir in the cream, ¼ cup cheese, Romano cheese, egg yolk, salt, pepper and nutmeg. Cook and stir over medium-low heat until a thermometer reads 160° (do not boil). Drain fettuccine; combine with Alfredo sauce and the remaining Parmesan cheese. If desired, sprinkle with parsley. **1 cup:** 907 cal., 73g fat (45g sat. fat), 290mg chol., 835mg sod., 45g carb. (5g sugars, 2g fiber), 23g pro.

**INSPIRED BY
OLIVE GARDEN**®
ALFREDO SAUCE

INSPIRED BY OLIVE GARDEN®
MARINARA DIPPING SAUCE

INSPIRED BY
PANERA®
MAC & CHEESE

COPYCAT MAC & CHEESE

My kids and I love mac and cheese. We always get it in the bread bowls when we're at Panera. With three cheeses, these white cheddar shells are a pretty close duplicate, if you ask us.
—*Steven Schend, Grand Rapids, MI*

TAKES: 25 MIN. • **MAKES:** 6 SERVINGS

3½ cups uncooked pipetti pasta, such as Barilla Pippetti, or medium pasta shells
¼ cup butter, cubed
¼ cup all-purpose flour
2½ cups 2% milk
¼ tsp. pepper
2 cups shredded white cheddar cheese
4 slices white American cheese, chopped
¼ cup grated Parmesan cheese
Bread bowls, optional

Cook pasta according to package directions; drain and set aside. In a large saucepan, melt butter over low heat; whisk in flour until smooth. Whisk in the milk and pepper. Bring to a boil; cook and stir for 2 minutes or until thickened. Stir in cheeses until melted; stir in pasta. Serve in bread bowls if desired.

1 cup: 538 cal., 27g fat (16g sat. fat), 79mg chol., 565mg sod., 50g carb. (7g sugars, 2g fiber), 23g pro.

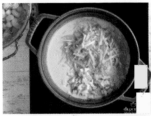

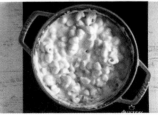

DID YOU KNOW?

When it comes to getting the smoothest cheese sauce possible, it's best to shred the cheese yourself. Give it a try and you'll see that it's well worth the extra effort. If you use store-bought shredded cheese, you may find your sauce has a little grittiness to it and the cheese may not melt completely. That's because some shredded cheeses contain cellulose, which helps cheese from clumping together in the bag.

TASTY TIPS

Give these ideas a shot when making the mac & cheese.
• Cubing the butter helps it melt evenly and quickly.
• A roux of flour and fat (butter) is the secret to this dish.
• Stir the cheese into the cream sauce until it's well melded.
• Make sure the pasta is completely covered with the cream sauce before serving.

OLIVE GARDEN FRIED LASAGNA

One of my favorite dishes at Olive Garden is their fried lasagna. On a whim,
I tried to re-create it at home. After a few tries, I think I got it pretty close to the original.

—Jolene Martinelli, Fremont, NH

PREP: 45 MIN. + FREEZING • **COOK:** 10 MIN./BATCH • **MAKES:** 10 SERVINGS

20 uncooked lasagna noodles
1 carton (32 oz.) whole-milk ricotta cheese
2½ cups shredded Italian cheese blend, divided
2 cups shredded part-skim mozzarella cheese
6 large eggs, beaten, divided use
4 tsp. Italian seasoning, divided
   Oil for deep-fat frying
2½ cups panko bread crumbs
1 jar (24 oz.) marinara sauce, warmed
1 jar (15 oz.) Alfredo sauce, warmed

WHY YOU'LL LOVE IT...

"This was amazing! Almost as easy as having to go to the restaurant to get them."
—RHIANNON464, TASTEOFHOME.COM

1. Cook lasagna noodles according to package directions for al dente. In a large bowl, combine ricotta, 1¼ cups Italian cheese blend, the mozzarella, 2 eggs and 3 tsp. Italian seasoning. Drain noodles. If desired, cut off ribboned edges (discard or save for another use). Spread about ¼ cup filling on each noodle. Starting with a short side, fold each in thirds. Place all on a parchment-lined baking sheet, seam side down. Freeze just until firm, about 1 hour.

2. In an electric skillet or deep fryer, heat oil to 375°. In a shallow bowl, mix bread crumbs, ⅔ cup Italian cheese blend and remaining 1 tsp. Italian seasoning. Place remaining 4 eggs in a separate shallow bowl. Dip lasagna bundles into eggs, then into crumb mixture, patting to help coating adhere.

3. Fry bundles in batches until golden brown, 8-10 minutes, turning once. Drain on paper towels. Serve bundles with the marinara, Alfredo, the remaining Italian cheese blend and, if desired, additional Italian seasoning.

2 lasagna rolls: 876 cal., 54g fat (19g sat. fat), 195mg chol., 1011mg sod., 61g carb. (11g sugars, 4g fiber), 37g pro.

INSPIRED BY
OLIVE GARDEN®
FRIED LASAGNA

INSPIRED BY
THE WIZARDING WORLD
OF HARRY POTTER™
UNIVERSAL ORLANDO
RESORT®

BUTTERBEER

FAVORITE
ODDS & ENDS

Turn here for copycat sides, sauces and sweets. You'll even find easy imitations of popular beverages, breads and more.

BACON PRETZEL FURY

I tried a bacon pretzel fury the last time I was at Busch Gardens, and afterward I ferociously tried to re-create it at home. I don't live anywhere close to the amusement park, so this version curbs my hankerings when back in the Midwest.

—*Alvin Ciepluch, Kenosha, WI*

PREP: 40 MIN. + RISING • **BAKE:** 15 MIN. • **MAKES:** 6 PRETZELS

12 thick-sliced bacon strips
1 pkg. (¼ oz.) active dry yeast
1½ cups warm water (110° to 115°)
2 Tbsp. sugar
2 Tbsp. butter, melted
1½ tsp. salt
4 to 4½ cups all-purpose flour
8 cups water
⅓ cup baking soda
1 large egg yolk
1 Tbsp. cold water
1 tsp. coarse salt
¼ cup butter, melted
6 wooden skewers

1. In a large skillet, cook bacon over medium heat until partially cooked but not crisp. Remove to paper towels to drain; set aside.

2. In a large bowl, dissolve yeast in warm water. Add sugar, butter, salt and 2 cups flour. Beat until smooth. Stir in enough remaining flour to form a soft dough (dough will be sticky).

3. Turn dough onto a floured surface; knead until smooth and elastic, 6-8 minutes. Place in a greased bowl, turning once to grease top. Cover and let rise in a warm place until doubled, about 1 hour.

4. Preheat oven to 425°. In a Dutch oven, bring 8 cups water and baking soda to a boil. Punch dough down; divide into 6 portions. Roll each portion into a 32-in. rope. Fold each rope in half, creating an upside-down V shape. Place 1 bacon strip over the top of each "V"; braid dough around the bacon, layering in a second bacon strip halfway. Pinch ends to seal; tuck under. Add to boiling water, 1 at a time; cook 30 seconds. Remove with 2 slotted spoons; drain on paper towels.

5. Place on greased baking sheets. Lightly beat egg yolk and cold water; brush over pretzels. Sprinkle with coarse salt. Bake until golden brown, 12-15 minutes. Brush with melted butter; sprinkle with additional coarse salt if desired. Remove from pans to wire racks. Insert skewers; serve warm.

1 pretzel: 533 cal., 21g fat (9g sat. fat), 61mg chol., 1699mg sod., 68g carb. (4g sugars, 3g fiber), 17g pro.

INSPIRED BY
BUSCH GARDENS®
BACON PRETZEL FURY

INSPIRED BY
CHICK-FIL-A®
*AVOCADO LIME
RANCH DRESSING*

AVOCADO LIME RANCH DRESSING

This avocado ranch dressing is a light take on a Chick-fil-A recipe. This version has no sugar added, is half the calories of the original, and is made with buttermilk, avocado, fresh cilantro and spices. Using freshly opened sour cream and buttermilk will help it last as long as possible.

—*Kelsey Reddick Smith, Knoxville, TN*

PREP: 15 MIN. + CHILLING • **MAKES:** 2 CUPS

½ cup buttermilk
½ cup sour cream
¼ cup mayonnaise
1 medium ripe avocado, peeled and cubed
2 Tbsp. chopped fresh cilantro
2 Tbsp. lime juice
1½ tsp. dill weed
½ tsp. salt
½ tsp. garlic powder
½ tsp. ground cumin
¼ tsp. pepper

Place all ingredients in a blender; cover and process until combined. Transfer to a jar. Refrigerate, covered, at least 1 hour before serving.

2 Tbsp.: 56 cal., 5g fat (1g sat. fat), 7mg chol., 109mg sod., 2g carb. (1g sugars, 1g fiber), 1g pro. **Diabetic exchanges:** 1 fat.

COPYCAT 57 SAUCE

This is a homemade version of our favorite steak sauce. We use it on everything from steaks, chicken, pork and burgers to fries. Excellent for basting grilled chicken or ribs, it's also a tasty addition to marinades.

—*Erin Wright, Wallace, KS*

TAKES: 20 MIN. • **MAKES:** 1½ CUPS

½ cup boiling water
½ cup raisins
⅔ cup ketchup
½ cup unsweetened applesauce
3 Tbsp. white vinegar
1 Tbsp. ground mustard
1 tsp. garlic powder
1 tsp. seasoned salt
1 tsp. chili powder
1 tsp. Worcestershire sauce
1 tsp. prepared yellow mustard

Pour boiling water over raisins in a small bowl; let stand 5 minutes. Drain. Transfer to a blender; add remaining ingredients. Cover and process until smooth. Strain if desired. Store in an airtight container in the refrigerator.

2 Tbsp.: 42 cal., 0 fat (0 sat. fat), 0 chol., 312mg sod., 10g carb. (8g sugars, 1g fiber), 1g pro.

INSPIRED BY HEINZ®
57 SAUCE

HOMEMADE SMILEY FRIES

These cute smiley fries take us back—back to a time with lunch tables, food trays and tiny milk cartons. If you were a hot-lunch kid growing up, there's a strong possibility that you were served smiley fries like these from the cafeteria line on more than one occasion.

—Lauren Habermehl, Pewaukee, WI

PREP: 45 MIN. • **COOK:** 5 MIN./BATCH • **MAKES:** 8 SERVINGS

2 cups mashed potatoes (without added milk and butter)
½ cup dry bread crumbs
2 Tbsp. cornstarch
½ tsp. salt
½ tsp. garlic powder
½ tsp. onion powder
¼ tsp. pepper
Oil for frying
Optional: Ketchup, mustard or ranch dressing

1. In a large bowl, stir together potatoes, bread crumbs, cornstarch and seasonings until smooth. On a lightly floured surface, roll out mixture to ¼-in. thickness. Cut with a floured 2-in. round cookie cutter, re-rolling scraps. Using a drinking straw, poke 2 circles into each round for eyes. Then, use a spoon to make a mouth.

2. In a large skillet or Dutch oven, heat ½ in. of oil to 350°. Fry rounds, a few at a time, until golden brown, 1-2 minutes on each side. Drain on paper towels; sprinkle with additional salt to taste. Serve warm with optional sauces.

6 fries: 131 cal., 7g fat (1g sat. fat), 0 chol., 208mg sod., 14g carb. (0 sugars, 2g fiber), 2g pro.

INSPIRED BY
MCCAIN

*SMILES®
MASHED
POTATO SHAPES*

INSPIRED BY
BOSTON MARKET®
*SWEET POTATO
CASSEROLE*

SWEET POTATO CASSEROLE

I make this classic for Thanksgiving, but I also have been known to serve it with meat loaf and even grilled meats.
—*Eleanor Sherry, Highland Park, IL*

PREP: 10 MIN. • **BAKE:** 25 MIN. • **MAKES:** 8 SERVINGS

CASSEROLE

- 2¼ to 2½ lbs. sweet potatoes, cooked, peeled and mashed (about 4 cups)
- ⅓ cup butter, melted
- 2 large eggs, lightly beaten
- ½ cup 2% milk
- 1 tsp. vanilla extract
- ½ cup sugar

TOPPING

- ½ cup chopped nuts
- ½ cup sweetened shredded coconut
- ½ cup packed brown sugar
- 3 Tbsp. butter, melted

1. In a large bowl, combine the mashed potatoes, butter, eggs, milk, vanilla and sugar. Spread mixture into a greased 1½-qt. casserole dish.

2. Combine topping ingredients and sprinkle over the potatoes. Bake at 375° until a thermometer reads 160°, about 25 minutes.
¾ cup: 445 cal., 21g fat (10g sat. fat), 80mg chol., 152mg sod., 62g carb. (42g sugars, 5g fiber), 6g pro.

COPY THAT!

Believe it or not, you can save a bit of time by using canned sweet potatoes to prepare this casserole. Drain the can of potatoes first, then mash the spuds with a potato masher or an electric mixer. If you're using canned sweet potatoes in syrup and you'd like to reduce the added sugar, simply rinse them well before mashing. Proceed with the recipe as directed.

THREE-CHEESE CREAMED SPINACH

Cream cheese, Parmesan and mozzarella make this dish wonderfully cheesy. Sprinkle it with french-fried onions before baking for a crisp boost of flavor.
—*Kathy Vazquez, Amarillo, TX*

TAKES: 20 MIN. • **MAKES:** 6 SERVINGS

- 2 pkg. (10 oz. each) frozen chopped spinach, thawed and squeezed dry
- 1½ cups spreadable chive and onion cream cheese
- 1 cup grated Parmesan cheese
- 1 cup shredded part-skim mozzarella cheese
- ¼ cup butter, cubed
- ¼ tsp. pepper

In a large saucepan, combine all ingredients. Cook and stir over medium heat for 8-10 minutes or until blended and mixture is heated through.
⅔ cup: 415 cal., 35g fat (23g sat. fat), 103mg chol., 685mg sod., 9g carb. (5g sugars, 3g fiber), 15g pro.

INSPIRED BY BOSTON MARKET®
CREAMED SPINACH

BUTTERBEER

Butterbeer is a beverage enjoyed by characters in the famed Harry Potter series by J.K. Rowling. Mentioned frequently throughout the books, this kid-friendly treat is described by Rowling as tasting a little bit like butterscotch and is served either hot or cold. Here's my take on the version that's served at the popular Harry Potter-themed amusement park.

—Lauren Habermehl, Pewaukee, WI

PREP: 20 MIN. + CHILLING • **MAKES:** 2 SERVINGS

BUTTERBEER FOAM

- ¼ cup hot water
- ½ cup marshmallow creme
- ½ envelope whipped topping mix (Dream Whip)
- 1 Tbsp. confectioners' sugar
- 1 pinch salt
- ½ tsp. butterscotch flavoring syrup
- ¼ tsp. butter extract
- ¼ tsp. caramel extract
- ⅛ tsp. vanilla extract

BUTTERBEER

- 2 cans (12 oz. each) cream soda, chilled
- 2 tsp. butterscotch flavoring syrup

1. In a large bowl, stir together hot water and marshmallow creme until smooth. Freeze until cool, 20-25 minutes. Stir in whipped topping mix, confectioners' sugar and salt; blend with a hand mixer 30-60 seconds or until foamy. Stir in butterscotch syrup and extracts.

2. Pour soda into two 16-oz. mugs; stir in butterscotch syrup. Top with Butterbeer Foam. Serve immediately.

1 serving: 351 cal., 2g fat (2g sat. fat), 0 chol., 138mg sod., 86g carb. (80g sugars, 0 fiber), 0 pro.

**INSPIRED BY
THE WIZARDING WORLD OF
HARRY POTTER™
UNIVERSAL ORLANDO
RESORT®**

BUTTERBEER

INSPIRED BY
BOSTON MARKET®
VEGETABLE STUFFING

GRANDMA'S CORNBREAD DRESSING

Growing up, we didn't have turkey. We had chicken, chopped and baked in my grandmother's dressing. Now we leave out the chicken and keep the cornbread dressing.
—*Suzanne Mohme, Bastrop, TX*

PREP: 40 MIN. + COOLING • **BAKE:** 45 MIN. • **MAKES:** 12 SERVINGS

1 cup all-purpose flour
1 cup cornmeal
2 tsp. baking powder
1 tsp. salt
2 large eggs, room temperature
1 cup buttermilk
¼ cup canola oil

DRESSING
1 Tbsp. canola oil
1 medium onion, chopped
2 celery ribs, chopped
3 large eggs
2 cans (10¾ oz. each) condensed cream of chicken soup, undiluted
3 tsp. poultry seasoning
1 tsp. pepper
½ tsp. salt
2 cups chicken broth

1. Preheat oven to 400°. In a large bowl, whisk flour, cornmeal, baking powder and salt. In another bowl, whisk eggs and buttermilk. Pour oil into an 8-in. ovenproof skillet; place skillet in oven 4 minutes.

2. Meanwhile, add the buttermilk mixture to flour mixture; stir just until moistened.

3. Carefully tilt and rotate skillet to coat bottom with oil; add batter. Bake 20-25 minutes or until a toothpick inserted in center comes out clean. Cool completely in pan on a wire rack.

4. Reduce oven setting to 350°. For dressing, in a large skillet, heat oil over medium-high heat. Add chopped onion and celery; cook and stir 4-6 minutes or until tender. Remove from heat. Coarsely crumble cornbread into skillet; toss to combine. In a small bowl, whisk eggs, condensed soup and seasonings; stir into bread mixture. Stir in broth.

5. Transfer to a greased 13x9-in. baking dish. Bake 45-55 minutes or until lightly browned.

⅔ cup: 236 cal., 12g fat (2g sat. fat), 83mg chol., 969mg sod., 25g carb. (2g sugars, 2g fiber), 7g pro.

RED ROASTED POTATOES

Some fragrant rosemary, fresh or dried, gives these potatoes a distinctive and subtle taste. This dish is simple to prepare, yet elegant in color and flavor. It's a wonderful addition to any menu.
—*Margie Wampler, Butler, PA*

TAKES: 30 MIN. • **MAKES:** 8 SERVINGS

2 lbs. small unpeeled red potatoes, cut into wedges
2 to 3 Tbsp. olive oil
2 garlic cloves, minced
1 Tbsp. minced fresh rosemary or 1 tsp. dried rosemary, crushed
½ tsp. salt
¼ tsp. pepper

1. Place potatoes in a 13x9-in. baking dish. Drizzle with the oil. Sprinkle with the garlic, rosemary, salt and pepper; toss gently to coat.

2. Bake at 450° until potatoes are golden brown and tender, 20-30 minutes.

1 cup: 114 cal., 4g fat (0 sat. fat), 0 chol., 155mg sod., 18g carb. (1g sugars, 2g fiber), 2g pro.

INSPIRED BY BOSTON MARKET®
ROTISSERIE POTATOES

FROZEN STRAWBERRY DAIQUIRIS

When I was in my early 20s, I went on a Carnival Cruise to the Caribbean. I got hooked on their frozen strawberry daiquiris and needed to come up with my own version. I think this is pretty darn close!

—*James Schend, Pleasant Prairie, WI*

TAKES: 10 MIN. • **MAKES:** 5 SERVINGS

1¼ cups rum
¾ cup frozen limeade
   concentrate, thawed
1 pkg. (15½ oz.) frozen
   sweetened sliced strawberries
2 to 2½ cups ice cubes
   Optional: Fresh strawberries
   and lime slices

In a blender, combine the rum, limeade concentrate, strawberries and ice. Cover and process until smooth and thickened (use more ice for thicker daiquiris). Pour into 5 cocktail glasses. If desired, garnish with fresh strawberries and lime slices.
1 cup: 299 cal., 0 fat (0 sat. fat), 0 chol., 7mg sod., 45g carb. (41g sugars, 2g fiber), 1g pro.

COPY THAT!

If you don't have frozen strawberries, you can try using fresh berries instead. It might make your frozen strawberry daiquiri slightly thinner, but you can always add more ice to balance it out. Otherwise, try using half frozen strawberries and half fresh, and settle on a ratio that creates an ideal drink.

DOLE WHIP

Your kitchen will be the happiest place on earth when you serve this sweet-sour treat. The recipe comes directly from the Disneyland app and tastes just like the real deal you'd order at the park.

—Taste of Home *Test Kitchen*

TAKES: 10 MIN. • **MAKES:** 2 SERVINGS

2 cups frozen pineapple chunks
1 cup vanilla ice cream
½ cup unsweetened pineapple
   juice

Place all ingredients in a blender; cover and process until thick, stopping and scraping sides as needed. Pour into a glass, topping with a swirl.
1 cup: 290 cal., 7g fat (4g sat. fat), 29mg chol., 87mg sod., 50g carb. (34g sugars, 1g fiber), 3g pro.

**INSPIRED BY
DISNEYLAND THEME PARK®**
DOLE WHIP

INSPIRED BY
CARNIVAL CRUISE LINES®
STRAWBERRY DAIQUIRIS

INSPIRED BY
CHEEZ-IT®
BAKED SNACK CRACKERS

HOMEMADE CHEEZ-ITS

Bring some of that childhood magic back to your kitchen with this recipe for homemade Cheez-Its.
It's a fun and delicious weekend baking project that the whole family can enjoy (and subsequently devour).
—*Lauren Habermehl, Pewaukee, WI*

PREP: 30 MIN. + CHILLING • **BAKE:** 15 MIN./BATCH + COOLING • **MAKES:** 12 DOZEN

---

8   oz. cheddar cheese, cubed
1   cup all-purpose flour
1   tsp. cornstarch
1   tsp. kosher salt
½   tsp. ground mustard
½   tsp. paprika
4   Tbsp. cold unsalted butter
2   Tbsp. ice water
1   large egg, beaten
    Flaky sea salt, optional

1. In a food processor, pulse cheese until finely chopped; transfer to a large bowl. Stir in flour, cornstarch, salt, mustard and paprika. Cut in butter until mixture resembles coarse crumbs. Gradually add ice water, tossing with a fork until dough holds together when pressed. Shape into a disk; wrap and refrigerate 1 hour or overnight.

2. Preheat oven to 350°. On a lightly floured surface, roll dough to a ⅛-in. thickness. Using a fluted pastry wheel, pizza cutter or sharp knife, cut dough into 1-in. squares. Transfer to parchment-lined baking sheets. Using a toothpick or skewer, poke a hole in center of each square. Brush with beaten egg; sprinkle with salt if desired.

3. Bake 15-18 minutes or until crisp and lightly golden around edges. Cool completely on baking sheets.

1 cracker: 13 cal., 1g fat (1g sat. fat), 2mg chol., 24mg sod., 1g carb. (0 sugars, 0 fiber), 0 pro.

PATIO PINTOS

Any time Mom had the gang over for dinner, she made these pinto beans. Once, she made a batch for my cousin's birthday and he ate the entire thing.
—*Joan Hallford, North Richland Hills, TX*

PREP: 25 MIN. • **BAKE:** 1 HOUR • **MAKES:** 10 SERVINGS

½ lb. bacon strips, chopped
1 large onion, chopped
2 garlic cloves, minced
6 cans (15 oz. each) pinto beans, rinsed and drained
4 cans (8 oz. each) tomato sauce
2 cans (4 oz. each) chopped green chiles
⅓ cup packed brown sugar
1 tsp. chili powder
¾ tsp. salt
½ tsp. dried oregano
¼ tsp. pepper

1. Preheat oven to 350°. In a Dutch oven, cook bacon over medium heat until crisp, stirring occasionally. Remove with a slotted spoon; drain on paper towels. Discard drippings, reserving 2 Tbsp. in pan.
2. Add onion to drippings; cook and stir over medium heat until tender, 6-8 minutes. Add the garlic; cook 1 minute longer. Stir in beans, tomato sauce, green chiles, brown sugar and seasonings. Sprinkle top with the bacon. Bake, covered, 60-70 minutes or until heated through.
Freeze option: Freeze cooled bean mixture in freezer containers. To use, partially thaw in refrigerator overnight. Heat through in a saucepan, stirring occasionally; add water if necessary.
¾ cup: 349 cal., 8g fat (2g sat. fat), 11mg chol., 1183mg sod., 55g carb. (13g sugars, 12g fiber), 17g pro.

COUNTRY TURNIP GREENS

If you've never tried making turnip greens, my recipe is an easy, tasty way to start. Pork and onions give the fresh greens wonderful flavor.
—*Sandi Pichon, Memphis, TN*

PREP: 20 MIN. • **COOK:** 45 MIN. • **MAKES:** 10 SERVINGS

¾ lb. lean salt pork or bacon, diced
4½ lbs. fresh turnip greens, trimmed
1½ cups water
1 large onion, chopped
1 tsp. sugar
¼ to ½ tsp. pepper

1. In a Dutch oven, cook salt pork until lightly browned. Drain, reserving 2 Tbsp. of drippings.
2. Stir the remaining ingredients into the reserved drippings. Bring to a boil. Reduce heat; cover and simmer for 45 minutes or until greens are tender.
Note: Fresh spinach can be substituted for the turnip greens. Just reduce the cooking time to 10 minutes or until the spinach is tender.
½ cup: 317 cal., 28g fat (10g sat. fat), 29mg chol., 622mg sod., 14g carb. (9g sugars, 4g fiber), 4g pro.

INSPIRED BY CRACKER BARREL®
TURNIP GREENS

INSPIRED BY
CRACKER BARREL®
PINTO BEANS

INSPIRED BY
LONG JOHN
SILVER'S®
HUSH PUPPIES

DOWN-HOME HUSH PUPPIES

Hush puppies are a classic southern side. The sweet-spicy flavor of these fried bites has delighted friends and family for decades.
—*Gene Pitts, Wilsonville, AL*

PREP: 15 MIN. + STANDING • **COOK:** 20 MIN. • **MAKES:** 2½ DOZEN

1 cup cornmeal
1 cup self-rising flour
1½ tsp. baking powder
½ tsp. salt
1 large onion, chopped
2 jalapeno peppers, seeded and diced
¼ cup sugar
1 large egg
1 cup buttermilk
Canola oil

1. In a large bowl, combine the first 7 ingredients. Add egg and buttermilk; stir just until moistened. Set aside at room temperature for 30 minutes. Do not stir again.

2. In an electric skillet or deep fryer, heat 2-3 in. of oil to 375°. Drop batter by rounded tablespoonfuls, a few at a time, into hot oil. Fry until golden brown, about 1½ minutes on each side. Drain on paper towels.

Note: As a substitute for 1 cup of self-rising flour, place 1½ tsp. baking powder and ½ tsp. salt in a measuring cup. Add all-purpose flour to measure 1 cup.

1 hush puppy: 73 cal., 3g fat (0 sat. fat), 7mg chol., 132mg sod., 10g carb. (2g sugars, 0 fiber), 1g pro.

COPYCAT RIB SHACK MASHED POTATOES

Idaho is well known for being the potato state—even our license plates say Famous Potatoes! This is my version of the scrumptious smashers that are served at a local barbecue joint. Everyone who tries them there begs for the recipe, which the place won't give out, so I made my own copycat version. These can be made ahead and kept warm in the slow cooker.

—Trisha Kruse, Eagle, ID

TAKES: 30 MIN. • **MAKES:** 12 SERVINGS

2½ lbs. potatoes, peeled and cubed
1 cup 2% milk, warmed
½ cup spreadable garlic and herb cream cheese
3 Tbsp. butter, softened
1 lb. bacon strips, cooked and crumbled
1 cup shredded cheddar cheese
½ cup shredded Parmesan cheese
3 green onions, chopped
2 Tbsp. minced fresh parsley or 2 tsp. dried parsley flakes
¼ tsp. salt
¼ tsp. pepper

Place potatoes in a Dutch oven; add water to cover. Bring to a boil. Reduce heat; cook, uncovered, until tender, 15-20 minutes. Drain and return to pan; gently mash potatoes while gradually adding the milk, cream cheese and butter to reach desired consistency. Stir in the remaining ingredients.

⅔ cup: 238 cal., 15g fat (8g sat. fat), 41mg chol., 477mg sod., 15g carb. (2g sugars, 1g fiber), 10g pro.

**INSPIRED BY
RIB SHACK®**

MASHED POTATOES

INSPIRED BY
CHICK-FIL-A®
CHICKEN NUGGETS

COPYCAT CHICK-FIL-A CHICKEN NUGGETS

I developed this recipe specifically to mimic our favorite restaurant's chicken nuggets.
The first time I made them I knew I had a winner: The whole family fought over who got the last one!
—*Jeni Pittard, Statham, GA*

PREP: 20 MIN. + MARINATING • **COOK:** 5 MIN./BATCH • **MAKES:** 8 SERVINGS

- 2 lbs. boneless skinless chicken breasts, cut into bite-sized pieces
- 1 Tbsp. dill pickle juice
- ½ cup cornstarch
- 1 Tbsp. soy sauce
- 1 large egg white
- ⅛ tsp. salt
- ⅛ tsp. pepper
- ¼ tsp. garlic powder
- ¼ tsp. paprika
- 1 Tbsp. Dijon mustard
  Oil for frying

1. In a bowl, add chicken pieces and dill pickle juice; toss to coat. Marinate at room temperature for 30 minutes. Meanwhile, combine the next 8 ingredients to form a thick batter. Add batter to the chicken mixture and toss to coat.

2. In a deep skillet or electric skillet, heat 1 in. oil to 375°. Fry chicken pieces, a few at a time, until browned and juices run clear, 1-2 minutes on each side. Drain on paper towels.

1 serving: 307 cal., 16g fat (2g sat. fat), 63mg chol., 514mg sod., 14g carb. (6g sugars, 0 fiber), 24g pro.

WHY YOU'LL LOVE IT...

"These copycat nuggets were so delicious. Don't let the thick batter worry you. Once it goes onto the chicken it thins out. So good! Keeping this in rotation."
—JUDY3990, TASTEOFHOME.COM

COPYCAT CHICK-FIL-A SAUCE

This sauce is a perfect at-home duplicate of a condiment my family
adores. It's great with chicken nuggets and even fries.
—*Jeni Pittard, Statham, GA*

TAKES: 5 MIN. • **MAKES:** ¾ CUP

- ¼ cup Dijon mustard
- 5 Tbsp. mayonnaise
- 3 Tbsp. barbecue sauce
- 3 Tbsp. honey

In a bowl, combine mustard, mayonnaise, barbecue sauce and honey.

2 Tbsp.: 132 cal., 8g fat (1g sat. fat), 4mg chol., 386mg sod., 12g carb. (11g sugars, 0 fiber), 0 pro.

**INSPIRED BY
CHICK-FIL-A®**
CHICK-FIL-A SAUCE

COPYCAT BURGER KING ONION RINGS

Burger King onion rings are satisfying in a way that french fries can't be—it's the texture. The crunch and flavor signal your brain to some sort of euphoria! Fortunately, it's possible to make a spot-on version at home. The King will be so proud.

—*Elizabeth King, Duluth, MN*

PREP: 20 MIN. • **COOK:** 5 MIN./BATCH • **MAKES:** 4 SERVINGS

1 large onion
1 cup all-purpose flour
1 tsp. baking powder
1 tsp. kosher salt
1 tsp. seasoned salt
1 large egg
½ cup whole milk
2 cups panko bread crumbs
Oil for deep-fat frying

1. Cut onion into ¼-in. slices; separate into rings. In a shallow bowl, combine flour, baking powder, salt and seasoned salt. In another shallow bowl, whisk egg and milk. Place bread crumbs in a third shallow bowl. Coat onion with flour mixture; dip in egg mixture, then dip in flour mixture and egg mixture again. Coat with bread crumbs, pressing to adhere.

2. In an electric skillet or deep fryer, heat oil to 375°. Fry onion rings, a few at a time, for 30 seconds on each side or until golden brown. Drain on paper towels. Sprinkle with additional seasoned salt.

1 serving: 158 cal., 8g fat (1g sat. fat), 33mg chol., 316mg sod., 18g carb. (3g sugars, 1g fiber), 4g pro.

SEASONED FRIES

Instead of making french fries from scratch, I reach for frozen spuds and make them my own with Parmesan cheese and Italian seasoning. They're always popular with my family and remind me of the seasoned fries I used to be able to get at Burger King.

—*Maribeth Edwards, Follansbee, WV*

TAKES: 15 MIN. • **MAKES:** 6 SERVINGS

6 cups frozen shoestring potatoes
½ cup grated Parmesan cheese
2 tsp. Italian seasoning
½ tsp. salt

Place shoestring potatoes on a foil-lined baking sheet. Bake at 450° for 8 minutes. Combine cheese, seasoning and salt; sprinkle over potatoes and mix gently. Bake 4-5 minutes longer or until the potatoes are browned and crisp.

¾ cup: 108 cal., 2g fat (1g sat. fat), 6mg chol., 344mg sod., 18g carb. (1g sugars, 3g fiber), 3g pro.

INSPIRED BY BURGER KING®
SEASONED FRIES

INSPIRED BY
BURGER
KING®
ONION RINGS

**INSPIRED BY
BURGER KING®**

*STRAWBERRY
SHAKE*

THICK STRAWBERRY SHAKES

Cool off with a thick and rich treat that will remind you of a malt shoppe!

—*Kathryn Conrad, Milwaukee, WI*

TAKES: 5 MIN. • **MAKES:** 2 SERVINGS

⅓ cup 2% milk
1½ cups vanilla ice cream
½ cup frozen unsweetened strawberries
1 Tbsp. strawberry preserves

In a blender, combine all ingredients; cover and process until smooth. Pour into chilled glasses; serve immediately.

1 cup: 257 cal., 12g fat (7g sat. fat), 47mg chol., 100mg sod., 35g carb. (28g sugars, 1g fiber), 5g pro.

COPY THAT!

Food historians believe ice cream originated in China, where people made it out of snow instead of cream or milk. To create a luscious treat that's rich in antioxidants, add some finely chopped dark chocolate to your shake.

MAKING MILKSHAKES

Consider these tips for masterful milkshakes:

• Pouring milk into the blender first helps combine all of the ingredients once you're ready to blend.
• Do not use heavy cream in your shakes. It will blend into little bits of butter.
• Use less milk for a thick shake, and more for a thinner shake.
• Softened ice cream works best. If the ice cream is too hard, you may end up adding more liquid to get the milkshake to blend properly.

COPYCAT RED LOBSTER CHEDDAR BAY BISCUITS

Here's my go-to recipe for biscuits. Brushing them with the garlic-butter topping before baking seals the deal!

—Amy Martin, Vancouver, WA

PREP: 25 MIN. • **BAKE:** 15 MIN. • **MAKES:** 1½ DOZEN

2½ cups all-purpose flour
3 tsp. baking powder
2 tsp. sugar
1 tsp. garlic powder
½ tsp. cream of tartar
¼ tsp. salt
¼ tsp. cayenne pepper
½ cup cold butter, cubed
1½ cups shredded cheddar cheese
¾ cup 2% milk
½ cup sour cream

TOPPING
6 Tbsp. butter, melted
1½ tsp. garlic powder
1 tsp. minced fresh parsley

1. Preheat oven to 450°. In a large bowl, whisk the first 7 ingredients. Cut in cold butter until mixture resembles coarse crumbs; stir in the cheese. Add milk and sour cream; stir just until moistened.

2. Drop by ¼ cupfuls 2 in. apart onto greased baking sheets. Mix the topping ingredients; brush over tops. Bake until light brown, 12-15 minutes. Serve warm.

1 biscuit: 206 cal., 14g fat (8g sat. fat), 36mg chol., 256mg sod., 15g carb. (2g sugars, 1g fiber), 5g pro.

INSPIRED BY
RED LOBSTER®

*CHEDDAR BAY
BISCUITS*

INSPIRED BY
OLIVE GARDEN®
CHICKEN MARGHERITA

GRILLED CHICKEN MARGHERITA

I've been making this dish for years. When I saw the same item on the menu at Olive Garden, I knew I had a winner. Fresh basil gets all the respect in this super supper.

—Judy Armstrong, Prairieville, LA

PREP: 25 MIN. + MARINATING • **GRILL:** 10 MIN. • **MAKES:** 4 SERVINGS

4 boneless skinless chicken breast halves (6 oz. each)
½ cup reduced-fat balsamic vinaigrette
3 garlic cloves, minced
½ tsp. salt
¼ tsp. pepper
¼ cup marinara sauce
16 fresh basil leaves
2 plum tomatoes, thinly sliced lengthwise
1 cup frozen artichoke hearts, thawed and chopped
3 green onions, chopped
¼ cup shredded part-skim mozzarella cheese

1. Flatten chicken to ½-in. thickness. In a large bowl, combine vinaigrette and garlic. Add chicken; turn to coat. Cover; refrigerate 30 minutes. Drain chicken, discarding marinade. Sprinkle chicken with salt and pepper.

2. On a lightly greased grill rack, grill chicken, covered, over medium heat or broil 4 in. from heat 5 minutes. Turn; top with marinara, basil, tomatoes, artichokes, onions and cheese. Cover and cook until chicken is no longer pink and cheese is melted, 5-6 minutes.

1 chicken breast: 273 cal., 8g fat (2g sat. fat), 98mg chol., 606mg sod., 10g carb. (4g sugars, 3g fiber), 38g pro. **Diabetic exchanges:** 5 lean meat, 1 vegetable, ½ fat.

INSPIRED BY
NOTHING
BUNDT CAKES®
*CHOCOLATE
CHOCOLATE CHIP
CAKE*

DOUBLE-TAKE DESSERTS

There's always room for dessert! Don't leave the house to enjoy your favorite sweet treats. Simply consider these no-fuss copycat bites instead!

THE FAMOUS DOUBLETREE COOKIE

We tested this recipe for family and friends, following every exact word. The hardest part? Waiting an hour to let the cookies sit on the baking pan. It was difficult but so worth the effort!

—Taste of Home *Test Kitchen*

PREP: 25 MIN. • **BAKE:** 20 MIN./BATCH + COOLING • **MAKES:** ABOUT 2½ DOZEN

1 cup butter, softened
¾ cup plus 1 Tbsp. sugar
¾ cup packed brown sugar
2 large eggs, room temperature
1¼ tsp. vanilla extract
¼ tsp. lemon juice
2¼ cups all-purpose flour
½ cup old-fashioned oats
1 tsp. baking soda
1 tsp. salt
   Dash ground cinnamon
2⅔ cups semisweet chocolate chips
1¾ cups chopped walnuts

1. Preheat oven to 300°. Cream butter and sugars until light and fluffy, 5-7 minutes. Beat in eggs, vanilla and lemon juice. Whisk together flour, oats, baking soda, salt and cinnamon. Fold into creamed mixture with chocolate chips and walnuts.

2. Drop dough by 3 tablespoonfuls 2 in. apart onto parchment-lined baking sheets. Bake until edges begin to brown and center is soft, 20-23 minutes. Cool on pans 1 hour until fully cooled and set.

1 cookie: 241 cal., 15g fat (7g sat. fat), 27mg chol., 167mg sod., 28g carb. (18g sugars, 2g fiber), 3g pro.

INSPIRED BY DOUBLETREE®

CHOCOLATE CHIP COOKIES

INSPIRED BY
CHEESECAKE FACTORY®
ORIGINAL CHEESECAKE

COPYCAT CHEESECAKE FACTORY ORIGINAL CHEESECAKE

If you're going to prepare cheesecake, why not re-create one of the most popular desserts in the country? It's easier than you think when you follow this four-step recipe.

—Taste of Home *Test Kitchen*

PREP: 30 MIN. + COOLING • **BAKE:** 1½ HOURS + CHILLING • **MAKES:** 16 SERVINGS

2½ cups graham cracker crumbs
¼ cup sugar
½ cup butter, melted

FILLING
4 pkg. (8 oz. each) cream cheese, softened
2 cups sour cream
1¾ cups sugar
1 Tbsp. vanilla extract
4 large eggs, room temperature, lightly beaten

TOPPING
1 cup sour cream
¼ cup sugar

1. Preheat oven to 325°. In a small bowl, combine graham cracker crumbs and sugar; stir in butter. Press onto the bottom and up the sides of a greased 9-in. springform pan. Place on a baking sheet. Bake until lightly browned, 18-22 minutes. Cool on a wire rack.

2. In a large bowl, beat cream cheese, sour cream, sugar and vanilla until smooth. Add eggs; beat on low speed just until combined. Pour into crust. Place pan on a double thickness of heavy-duty foil (about 18 in. square). Securely wrap foil around pan.

3. Place in a larger baking pan; add 1 in. hot water to larger pan. Bake until center is just set and top appears dull, about 1½ hours. Remove springform pan from water bath. Let stand 5 minutes on a wire rack.

4. For topping, in a small bowl, mix sour cream and sugar; spread over top of cheesecake. Bake 5 minutes longer without water bath. Cool 10 minutes on wire rack. Loosen sides from pan with a knife; remove foil. Cool 1 hour longer. Refrigerate overnight, covering when completely cooled. Remove rim from pan.

1 piece: 536 cal., 37g fat (21g sat. fat), 151mg chol., 329mg sod., 45g carb. (36g sugars, 1g fiber), 8g pro.

PLATE LIKE A PRO

A hot knife is the secret to cutting nice, tidy slices of cake and cheesecake. You'll need a sharp knife, some hot water and a towel. Dip the blade into water to heat, then wipe dry and cut. Repeat each time for pretty slices with clean edges.

CREAM-FILLED CUPCAKES

These chocolate cupcakes have a fun filling and shiny chocolate frosting
that make them extra special. They always disappear in a flash!

—Kathy Kittell, Lenexa, KS

PREP: 20 MIN. • **BAKE:** 15 MIN. + COOLING • **MAKES:** 2 DOZEN

1 pkg. devil's food cake mix
  (regular size)
2 tsp. hot water
¼ tsp. salt
1 jar (7 oz.) marshmallow creme
½ cup shortening
⅓ cup confectioners' sugar
½ tsp. vanilla extract

GANACHE FROSTING
1 cup semisweet chocolate chips
¾ cup heavy whipping cream

1. Prepare and bake cake batter according to package directions, using 24 paper-lined muffin cups. Cool for 5 minutes before removing from pans to wire racks to cool completely.

2. For filling, in a small bowl, combine water and salt until salt is dissolved. Cool. In a small bowl, beat the marshmallow creme, shortening, confectioners' sugar and vanilla until light and fluffy, 3-4 minutes; beat in the salt mixture.

3. Transfer cream filling to a pastry bag fitted with a round pastry tip. Push tip through the top of each cupcake to fill center.

4. Place chocolate chips in a small bowl. In a small saucepan, bring cream just to a boil. Pour over chocolate; whisk until smooth. Cool, stirring occasionally, to room temperature or until ganache reaches a dipping consistency.

5. Dip cupcake tops in ganache; chill for 20 minutes or until set. Store in the refrigerator.

1 cupcake: 262 cal., 15g fat (5g sat. fat), 32mg chol., 223mg sod., 29g carb. (20g sugars, 1g fiber), 2g pro.

INSPIRED BY
CALIFORNIA PIZZA KITCHEN®
BUTTER CAKE

CALIFORNIA PIZZA KITCHEN BUTTER CAKE

I love dining at California Pizza Kitchen and was wondering if there was a way I could get my hands on the butter cake recipe—which, by the way, is to die for. With a few attempts, I think I got the recipe perfect.
—*Madeeha Anwar (bakecellence.com), Woodbridge, VA*

PREP: 25 MIN. • **BAKE:** 35 MIN. • **MAKES:** 8 SERVINGS

1 Tbsp. plus 1 cup sugar
1 cup butter, room temperature
1 tsp. vanilla extract
1 tsp. almond extract
3 large eggs, room temperature
1½ cups all-purpose flour
1 tsp. baking powder
1 cup buttermilk,
   room temperature
   Vanilla ice cream, optional

1. Preheat oven to 375°. Line bottom of a greased 9-in. round baking pan with parchment; grease paper. Dust bottom and sides with 1 Tbsp. sugar.

2. In a large bowl, beat butter, remaining 1 cup sugar and extracts until light and fluffy, 5-7 minutes. Add eggs, 1 at a time, beating well after each addition. In another bowl, whisk flour and baking powder; add to creamed mixture alternately with buttermilk, beating well after each addition.

3. Transfer to prepared pan. Bake until a toothpick inserted in center comes out clean, 35-40 minutes. Cool 5 minutes before transferring to a wire rack to cool completely. If desired, serve with ice cream.

1 piece: 319 cal., 25g fat (15g sat. fat), 131mg chol., 210mg sod., 18g carb. (0 sugars, 1g fiber), 5g pro.

CHOCOLATE PEANUT BUTTER SHAKES

These rich chocolate peanut butter shakes will make you feel as if you're sitting in a 1950s soda fountain. Make it modern with an over-the-top garnish like skewered doughnut holes, chocolate-dipped cookies or fluffernutter sandwich squares.
—*Taste of Home Test Kitchen*

TAKES: 10 MIN. • **MAKES:** 2 SERVINGS

¾ cup 2% milk
1½ cups chocolate ice cream
¼ cup creamy peanut butter
2 Tbsp. chocolate syrup
   Optional toppings: Sweetened
   whipped cream; miniature
   peanut butter cups, quartered;
   and additional chocolate syrup

In a blender, combine the milk, ice cream, peanut butter and syrup; cover and process until smooth. If desired, garnish servings with whipped cream, peanut butter cups and additional chocolate syrup.

1 cup: 501 cal., 29g fat (11g sat. fat), 41mg chol., 262mg sod., 51g carb. (43g sugars, 3g fiber), 14g pro.

INSPIRED BY DAIRY QUEEN®

REESE'S PEANUT BUTTER CUP BLIZZARD TREAT

COPYCAT CELEBRATION CHEESECAKE

Both my children were born on the same day five years apart, so I like to make an elaborate dessert to celebrate the occasion. This seven-layered beauty really fits the bill. The baking and preparation are easy, but you do need to set aside some time for the assembly. Everyone will be amazed when they see the final product.

—*Kristyne McDougle Walter, Lorain, OH*

PREP: 1 HOUR + FREEZING • **BAKE:** 30 MIN. + COOLING • **MAKES:** 16 SERVINGS

4 cups cold 2% milk

3 pkg. (3.4 oz. each) instant white chocolate pudding mix

1 pkg. white cake mix (regular size)

1⅓ cups rainbow sprinkles, divided

1 pkg. (1 oz.) freeze-dried strawberries

3 to 12 drops blue food coloring

¼ cup baking cocoa

2 cartons (24.3 oz. each) ready-to-serve cheesecake filling

2 cans (16 oz. each) cream cheese frosting

2 Tbsp. rainbow sequin sprinkles

1. Preheat oven to 350°. In each of 3 small bowls, whisk 1⅓ cups milk and 1 package pudding mix for 2 minutes. Refrigerate, covered, while baking cake layers.

2. Line bottoms of 2 greased 9-in. round baking pans with parchment; grease paper. Prepare cake mix batter according to package directions, folding ⅔ cup sprinkles into batter. Transfer to prepared pans. Bake and cool as package directs.

3. Using a long serrated knife, trim tops of cake layers to level. Crumble trimmings; transfer to a parchment-lined baking sheet. Bake at 350° until crisp but not browned, about 5 minutes. Cool completely on pan on wire rack.

4. Line two 9-in. springform pans with plastic, letting ends extend over sides. Place strawberries in a food processor; process until ground. Stir ground strawberries into 1 bowl of pudding. To another bowl of pudding, whisk in blue food coloring. To the third bowl, whisk in cocoa; refrigerate chocolate pudding.

5. Place 1 cake layer in 1 prepared springform pan; spread with the strawberry pudding. Place remaining cake layer in remaining prepared springform pan; spread with blue pudding. Freeze both pans at least 1 hour. Top each with 1 carton cheesecake filling. Freeze at least 1 hour.

6. Remove strawberry-layered pan from freezer; spread chocolate pudding over top. Return to freezer for 3 hours. Meanwhile, stir remaining ⅔ cup sprinkles into cooled cake crumbs.

7. Remove rims from springform pans; discard plastic. Place strawberry-layered cake on a serving plate; top with blue-layered cake. Frost top and sides with cream cheese frosting. Gently press crumb mixture into frosting on sides of cake; sprinkle with sequins. Freeze until ready to serve. Remove 10 minutes before cutting.

1 piece: 871 cal., 43g fat (19g sat. fat), 120mg chol., 929mg sod., 114g carb. (90g sugars, 1g fiber), 9g pro.

CHEESECAKE FACTORY®
CELEBRATION CHEESECAKE

INSPIRED BY
KLONDIKE BARS®
KLONDIKE BARS

HOMEMADE ICE CREAM SANDWICHES

Why settle for store-bought ice cream sandwiches when you can
have ones that taste even better and aren't that difficult to make?

—Kea Fisher, Bridger, MT

PREP: 25 MIN. + FREEZING • **BAKE:** 10 MIN. + COOLING • **MAKES:** 16 SANDWICHES

1   **pkg. chocolate cake mix
(regular size)**
¼   **cup shortening**
¼   **cup butter, softened**
1   **large egg**
1   **Tbsp. water**
1   **tsp. vanilla extract**
½   **gallon ice cream**

WHY YOU'LL LOVE IT...

*"These are great! Better
than those in the store. Didn't
last long at my house, and
there are only two of us!
My husband is already
wanting more."*
—JANLECK, TASTEOFHOME.COM

1. In a large bowl, combine the cake mix, shortening, butter, egg,
water and vanilla until well blended. Divide into 4 equal parts.
2. Between waxed paper, roll 1 part into a 10x6-in. rectangle. Remove
top piece of waxed paper and invert dough onto a ungreased baking
sheet. Remove second piece of waxed paper. Score the dough into
8 pieces, each 3x2½ in. Repeat with remaining dough.
3. Bake at 350° until puffed, 8-10 minutes. Immediately cut along
the scored lines and prick holes in each piece with a fork. Cool on
wire racks.
4. Cut ice cream into 16 slices, each 3x2½x1 in. Place ice cream slice
between 2 chocolate cookies; wrap in waxed paper or another wrap.
Freeze on a baking sheet overnight. May be frozen for up to 2 months.
1 sandwich: 315 cal., 15g fat (8g sat. fat), 48mg chol., 321mg sod., 42g
carb. (28g sugars, 1g fiber), 4g pro.

GIRL SCOUT COOKIES

To commemorate the anniversary of the first nationwide sale, the Girl Scouts are pleased to share the original sugar cookie recipe used when the troops made their own cookies.

—Girl Scout Council

PREP: 15 MIN. + CHILLING • **BAKE:** 10 MIN./BATCH • **MAKES:** 4 DOZEN (2½-IN. COOKIES)

1 cup butter, softened
1 cup sugar
2 large eggs, room temperature
2 Tbsp. milk
1 tsp. vanilla extract
2½ cups all-purpose flour
2 tsp. baking powder
Decorator's sugar, optional

1. In a bowl, cream the butter and sugar until light and fluffy, 5-7 minutes. Add eggs, 1 at a time, beating well after each addition. Beat in milk and vanilla. Whisk together flour and baking powder; gradually add to the creamed mixture and mix well. Chill at least 2 hours or overnight.

2. Preheat oven to 350°. On a lightly floured surface, roll the dough to ¼-in. thickness. Cut with 2½-in. round, trefoil or other cookie cutter of your choice. Place cookies on ungreased baking sheets. Sprinkle with decorator's sugar if desired.

3. Bake until lightly browned, 8-10 minutes. Cool on wire racks.

1 cookie: 78 cal., 4g fat (3g sat. fat), 18mg chol., 54mg sod., 9g carb. (4g sugars, 0 fiber), 1g pro.

COPY THAT!

If you plan to freeze these, arrange the cooled treats in a single layer on a baking sheet, and set the sheet in the freezer for 30 minutes or until the cookies are frozen. Layer the frozen cookies in airtight containers, with a piece of parchment or waxed paper separating layers. Freeze for up to 3 months. When it's time to enjoy the cookies, let them thaw at room temperature or heat them in the microwave for a few seconds before serving.

INSPIRED BY
GIRL SCOUT COUNCIL®
GIRL SCOUT COOKIES

INSPIRED BY
NOTHING
BUNDT CAKES®

*CHOCOLATE
CHOCOLATE CHIP
CAKE*

COPYCAT NOTHING BUNDT CAKE

My kids love chocolate cake so I'm always looking for away to kick it up a little.
This recipe is so moist and delicious—and so easy to make. The kids love it.

—Elizabeth Wynne, Aztec, NM

PREP: 15 MIN. • **COOK:** 40 MIN. • **MAKES:** 16 SERVINGS

---

1 pkg. devil's food cake mix (regular size)

1 pkg. (3.9 oz.) instant chocolate pudding mix

1 cup sour cream

½ cup canola oil

½ cup water

4 large eggs, room temperature

3 tsp. vanilla extract

1 cup semisweet chocolate chips

FROSTING

1 pkg. (8 oz.) cream cheese, softened

¼ cup butter, softened

1½ tsp. vanilla extract

3 cups confectioners' sugar

1. Preheat oven to 350°. Grease and flour a 10-in. fluted tube pan.

2. In a large bowl, combine the first 7 ingredients; beat on low speed 30 seconds. Beat on medium 2 minutes. Stir in chocolate chips. Transfer to prepared pan. Bake until a toothpick inserted near the center comes out clean, 35-40 minutes. Cool in pan 10 minutes before removing to a wire rack to cool completely.

3. In a large bowl, beat cream cheese, butter and vanilla until smooth. Gradually beat in confectioners' sugar. Pipe or spread over top of cake.

1 piece: 460 cal., 23g fat (10g sat. fat), 79mg chol., 370mg sod., 61g carb. (44g sugars, 1g fiber), 5g pro.

BOURBON & CORNFLAKES ICE CREAM

Humphry Slocombe's Secret Breakfast is a rich vanilla ice cream infused with bourbon.
Crunchy, golden brown cornflake cookies are swirled within. I came up
with the recipe for friends who couldn't find Humphry Slocombe ice cream.
—*Andrea Potischman, Menlo Park, CA*

PREP: 45 MIN. + CHILLING • **PROCESS:** 30 MIN. + FREEZING • **MAKES:** 1 QT.

3 Tbsp. heavy whipping cream
3 Tbsp. unsalted butter, melted
2 Tbsp. sugar
  Dash salt
1½ cups cornflakes, coarsely
  crushed

VANILLA BOURBON ICE
  CREAM
5 large egg yolks
½ cup sugar
  Dash salt
1 cup whole milk
1½ cups heavy whipping cream
1 tsp. vanilla extract
3 Tbsp. bourbon

1. Preheat oven to 375°. In a small bowl, combine the cream, butter, sugar and salt. Stir in cornflakes until well coated. Spread onto a parchment-lined baking sheet. Bake until golden brown, 12-15 minutes, stirring once. Cool completely.

2. For the ice cream, in a large heavy saucepan, whisk egg yolks, sugar and salt until blended; stir in milk. Cook over low heat until mixture is just thick enough to coat a metal spoon and a thermometer reads at least 160°, stirring constantly. Do not allow to boil. Remove from heat immediately.

3. Quickly transfer to a small bowl; place bowl in a pan of ice water. Stir gently and occasionally for 2 minutes. Stir in cream and vanilla. Press waxed paper onto surface of custard. Refrigerate several hours or overnight.

4. Stir bourbon into custard. Fill cylinder of ice cream maker no more than two-thirds full; freeze according to manufacturer's directions, adding the cornflakes during the last 2 minutes of processing. (Refrigerate any remaining mixture until ready to freeze.)

5. Transfer ice cream to freezer containers, allowing headspace for expansion. Freeze until firm, 2-4 hours.

½ cup: 353 cal., 26g fat (16g sat. fat), 187mg chol., 108mg sod., 23g carb. (19g sugars, 0 fiber), 5g pro.

INSPIRED BY
HUMPHRY
SLOCOMBE®

*SECRET
BREAKFAST
ICE CREAM*

INSPIRED BY
IT'S-IT ICE CREAM®
ICE CREAM SANDWICH

ALMOST IT'S-IT ICE CREAM SANDWICHES

You'll discover why this treat is so popular in San Francisco. It's snack heaven—
ice cream, delicious oatmeal cookies and a touch of chocolate.

—Jacyn Siebert, San Francisco, CA

PREP: 40 MIN. + FREEZING • **BAKE:** 15 MIN./BATCH + COOLING • **MAKES:** 7 SERVINGS

½ cup butter, softened
¾ cup packed brown sugar
¼ cup sugar
1 large egg, room temperature
½ tsp. vanilla extract
¾ cup all-purpose flour
½ tsp. baking soda
½ tsp. ground cinnamon
¼ tsp. baking powder
¼ tsp. salt
1½ cups quick-cooking oats
¼ cup chopped raisins, optional

ASSEMBLY

3 cups vanilla ice cream
1 bottle (7¼ oz.) chocolate hard-shell ice cream topping
   Optional: Sprinkles, chopped nuts and miniature semisweet chocolate chips

1. Preheat oven to 350°. In a large bowl, cream butter and sugars until light and fluffy, 5-7 minutes. Beat in egg and vanilla. In another bowl, whisk flour, baking soda, cinnamon, baking powder and salt; gradually beat into creamed mixture. Stir in oats and, if desired, raisins.

2. Shape into fourteen 1¼-in. balls; place 2½ in. apart on ungreased baking sheets. Bake until golden brown, roughly 11-13 minutes. Cool on pans 3 minutes. Remove to wire racks to cool completely.

3. To assemble ice cream sandwiches, place ⅓ cup ice cream on bottom of a cookie. Top with a second cookie, pressing gently to flatten ice cream; place on a baking sheet. Repeat with remaining cookies and ice cream. Freeze until firm.

4. Remove ice cream sandwiches from the freezer. Working over a small bowl, drizzle chocolate topping over half of each sandwich, allowing excess to drip off. If desired, roll the other half's edge in sprinkles, nuts or chocolate chips.

5. Place on a waxed paper-lined baking sheet; freeze until serving. Wrap individually and place in a freezer container for longer storage.

1 ice cream sandwich: 580 cal., 29g fat (16g sat. fat), 86mg chol., 364mg sod., 74g carb. (50g sugars, 3g fiber), 7g pro.

COPY THAT!

One of the joys of making your own ice cream sandwiches is that you can use any ice cream flavor you like! These oatmeal cookies would work really well with butter-pecan ice cream, coffee ice cream or even the homemade bourbon-cornflakes ice cream from p. 236.

HOMEMADE OREO COOKIES

An embossing rolling pin, if you have one, helps you quickly make these cookies with a whimsical design.
—*Christine Rukavena, Milwaukee, WI*

PREP: 40 MIN. + CHILLING • **BAKE:** 10 MIN./BATCH + COOLING • **MAKES:** 3 DOZEN

¾ cup unsalted butter, softened
1 cup sugar
⅓ cup packed brown sugar
1 large egg, room temperature
1 large egg yolk, room temperature
1¼ tsp. vanilla extract
1⅔ cups all-purpose flour
1 cup baking cocoa
½ tsp. salt
½ tsp. baking powder
2 to 3 tsp. hot brewed coffee, optional

FILLING

⅓ cup shortening
⅓ cup unsalted butter, softened
1¼ tsp. vanilla extract
2¼ cups confectioners' sugar
⅓ cup marshmallow creme

1. In a mixing bowl, cream butter and sugars until light and fluffy, 5-7 minutes. Beat in egg, yolk and vanilla. Sift together flour, cocoa, salt and baking powder. Gradually add to creamed mixture.

2. Divide dough in half; roll each between sheets of floured parchment into 8-in. disks. Refrigerate 30 minutes or until firm enough to roll.

3. Preheat oven to 325°. Roll each portion of dough directly on parchment-lined baking sheets to ⅛-in. thickness. If using an embossing pin, brush embossing pin with cocoa to prevent sticking; roll pin over dough to transfer design.

4. Cut with a floured 2-in. round cookie cutter, leaving at least ½ in. between cookies. Remove trimmings. (If dough becomes too soft, chill as needed.)

5. If desired, combine 3 Tbsp. dough and enough hot coffee to reach piping consistency; transfer thinned dough to a pastry bag fitted with a #1 round tip, and decorate cutouts as desired.

6. Bake 10-12 minutes or until firm. Cool on pans 2 minutes. Remove to wire racks to cool completely.

7. For filling, beat the shortening, butter and vanilla until blended. Gradually beat in confectioners' sugar and marshmallow creme until smooth. Spread filling on bottoms of half the cookies; cover with remaining cookies. Store in an airtight container.

1 sandwich cookie: 159 cal., 8g fat (4g sat. fat), 25mg chol., 44mg sod., 22g carb. (16g sugars, 1g fiber), 1g pro.

INSPIRED BY
OREO®
OREO COOKIES

INSPIRED BY
WILLIAMS-SONOMA®
PEPPERMINT BARK

PEPPERMINT BARK

After sampling peppermint bark from Williams-Sonoma, I thought, *I can make that!* Using four ingredients, I came up with a simple version that won over my friends and family.
—*Patti Maurer, Wise, VA*

PREP: 15 MIN. + CHILLING • **MAKES:** 1½ LBS. (24 SERVINGS)

1 tsp. plus 3 Tbsp. shortening, divided
1 pkg. (10 oz.) Andes creme de menthe baking chips
2 cups white baking chips
½ cup crushed peppermint candies

1. Line a 13x9-in. pan with foil; grease foil with 1 tsp. shortening.

2. In a microwave, melt Andes baking chips and 1 Tbsp. shortening; stir until smooth. Pour into prepared pan. Refrigerate 10 minutes or until set.

3. In top of a double boiler or a metal bowl over barely simmering water, melt baking chips with remaining shortening; stir until smooth. Spread over chocolate layer; sprinkle with crushed candies. Cool. Refrigerate 2 hours or until firm.

4. Break into small pieces. Store in an airtight container.

1 oz.: 161 cal., 10g fat (7g sat. fat), 3mg chol., 19mg sod., 17g carb. (16g sugars, 0 fiber), 1g pro.

CONTEST-WINNING MOIST CHOCOLATE CAKE

You don't have to spend a lot of time to serve an elegant and delicious dessert.
You can quickly mix up the batter in one bowl, bake the cake and serve a crowd.

—Christa Hageman, Telford, PA

PREP: 15 MIN. • **BAKE:** 45 MIN. + COOLING • **MAKES:** 12 SERVINGS

2 cups sugar
1¾ cups all-purpose flour
¾ cup baking cocoa
2 tsp. baking soda
1 tsp. baking powder
1 tsp. salt
2 large eggs, room temperature
1 cup strong brewed coffee
1 cup buttermilk
½ cup canola oil
1 tsp. vanilla extract
1 Tbsp. confectioners' sugar

1. In a large bowl, combine the first 6 ingredients. Add the eggs, coffee, buttermilk, oil and vanilla; beat on medium speed for 2 minutes (batter will be thin). Pour into a greased and floured 10-in. fluted tube pan.

2. Bake at 350° for 45-50 minutes or until a toothpick inserted in the center comes out clean. Cool for 10 minutes before removing from pan to a wire rack to cool completely. Dust with confectioners' sugar.

Note: To substitute for each cup of buttermilk, use 1 Tbsp. white vinegar or lemon juice plus enough milk to measure 1 cup. Stir, then let stand 5 min. Or, use 1 cup plain yogurt or 1¾ tsp. cream of tartar plus 1 cup milk.

1 slice: 315 cal., 11g fat (2g sat. fat), 36mg chol., 473mg sod., 52g carb. (34g sugars, 1g fiber), 5g pro.

COPY THAT!

Moist and soft cake comes down to the fat(s) used. In general, cakes that are made using cooking oil (vegetable, canola or grapeseed) tend to be moister and softer than cakes made with butter or shortening. This chocolate cake combines canola oil with buttermilk, which, with its acidic quality, breaks down the gluten in the flour and also adds to the cake's moist texture.

INSPIRED BY
KFC®
CHOCOLATE CHIP CAKE

INSPIRED BY
GIRL SCOUTS COUNCIL®
*TREFOIL SHORTBREAD
COOKIES*

SHORTBREAD

I live in Missouri, but many of our family recipes come from New Zealand, where I lived as a youngster. I proudly lay claim to a Down Under heritage! These special-occasion cookies bring back warm memories of my childhood, and I'm going to make sure they're passed on to the next generation in my family no matter where they live.

—*A. Swenson, Camdenton, MO*

PREP: 15 MIN. + CHILLING • **BAKE:** 10 MIN./BATCH • **MAKES:** 5 DOZEN

- 1 cup butter, softened
- ½ cup sugar
- ½ cup confectioners' sugar
- 2 cups all-purpose flour
- ½ cup cornstarch
- ½ tsp. salt

1. In large bowl, cream butter and sugars until light and fluffy, 5-7 minutes. Combine flour, cornstarch and salt; gradually add to creamed mixture and mix well. Roll dough into a 15x2x1-in. rectangle; chill.

2. Preheat oven to 325°. Cut dough into ¼-in. slices; place 2 in. apart on ungreased baking sheets. Prick with a fork. Bake 10-12 minutes or until set. Remove to wire racks to cool.

1 cookie: 57 cal., 3g fat (2g sat. fat), 8mg chol., 44mg sod., 7g carb. (3g sugars, 0 fiber), 0 pro.

COPY THAT!

Poking small holes in the dough allows some steam to escape while baking, preventing bubbles inside the cookies. This results in a far more uniform texture throughout the shortbread.

BLACK TIE CHOCOLATE MOUSSE CAKE

To slice this incredible cake, run a sharp knife under hot water and dry. Cut the first slice.
Rinse the knife under hot water and dry. Repeat with every slice.
—Taste of Home *Test Kitchen*

PREP: 1½ HOURS + CHILLING • **BAKE:** 25 MIN. + COOLING • **MAKES:** 16 SERVINGS

½ cup baking cocoa
1 cup boiling water
½ cup butter, softened
1 cup sugar
2 large eggs, room temperature
¾ tsp. vanilla extract
1⅓ cups all-purpose flour
1 tsp. baking soda
¼ tsp. baking powder
¼ tsp. salt

CHOCOLATE CHEESECAKE

4 oz. cream cheese, softened
¼ cup confectioners' sugar
½ tsp. vanilla extract
½ cup dark chocolate chips, melted and slightly cooled
½ cup heavy whipping cream

WHITE CHOCOLATE MOUSSE

1 cup heavy whipping cream
2 Tbsp. sugar
3 oz. cream cheese, softened
3 oz. white baking chocolate, melted and cooled

GANACHE

3 cups semisweet chocolate chips
1½ cups heavy whipping cream

GARNISH

2 cups miniature semisweet chocolate chips
¼ cup white baking chips, melted

1. Preheat oven to 350°. In a small bowl, combine cocoa and water; set aside to cool completely. In a large bowl, cream butter and sugar until light and fluffy, 5-7 minutes. Add eggs, 1 at a time, beating well after each addition. Beat in vanilla. Whisk together flour, baking soda, baking powder and salt; add to creamed mixture alternately with cocoa mixture, beating well after each addition.
2. Pour into a greased parchment-lined 9-in. round baking pan. Bake until a toothpick inserted in the center comes out clean, 25-30 minutes. Cool for 10 minutes before removing from pan to a wire rack to cool completely.
3. For chocolate cheesecake layer, in a small bow, beat cream cheese, confectioners' sugar and vanilla until smooth. Beat in cooled melted dark chocolate until combined. In another bowl, beat cream until soft peaks form. Fold into cream cheese mixture. Place cake layer in bottom of a 9-in. springform pan; spread cheesecake over top. Refrigerate until chilled, about 1 hour.
4. For white chocolate mousse, in a bowl beat the cream until it begins to thicken. Gradually add sugar, beating until stiff peaks form; set aside. In another bowl, beat cream cheese until fluffy. Add the white chocolate and beat until smooth. Fold in whipped cream. Spread over chocolate cheesecake layer. Refrigerate until set and chilled, about 1 hour.
5. For ganache, place chips in a large bowl. In a small saucepan, bring cream just to a boil. Pour over chocolate; stir with a whisk until smooth.
6. Cool slightly, stirring occasionally. Reserve ¾ cup for frosting; cover and refrigerate until cold.
7. Remove cake from pan; place on a wire rack. Pour remaining ganache over cake, allowing it to coat sides. For garnish, press miniature chocolate chips into sides of cake. Drizzle melted white chips over top. Refrigerate, covered, until chilled. Beat reserved ganache until piping consistency, about 15 seconds. Pipe around top edge. Refrigerate until serving.

1 piece: 696 cal., 48g fat (29g sat. fat), 102mg chol., 241mg sod., 71g carb. (56g sugars, 4g fiber), 8g pro.

**INSPIRED BY
OLIVE GARDEN®**

*BLACK TIE
CHOCOLATE
MOUSSE CAKE*

INSPIRED BY
CRACKER BARREL®
FRUIT COBBLER

FRESH FRUIT COBBLER

I received this recipe years ago. It's a family favorite, especially when Maine blueberries are in season. What a treat on a hot summer day!

—*Paula Chick, Lewiston, ME*

PREP: 15 MIN. • **BAKE:** 40 MIN. • **MAKES:** 12 SERVINGS

5 to 6 cups chopped fresh fruit (apples, rhubarb, blueberries or peaches)
2 cups all-purpose flour
½ cup sugar
4 tsp. baking powder
1 tsp. salt
½ cup cold butter, cubed
1 cup 2% milk

TOPPING

⅔ cup sugar
¼ cup cornstarch
1½ cups boiling water

1. Preheat oven to 350°. Arrange fruit evenly in the bottom of a 13x9-in. greased baking dish.
2. In a bowl, combine flour, sugar, baking powder and salt; cut in butter until crumbly. Stir in milk. Spoon over fruit. Combine sugar and cornstarch; sprinkle over batter. Pour water over all. Bake until fruit is tender and topping is golden, 40-45 minutes.

Note: If desired, a combination of apples and rhubarb or blueberries and peaches can be used.

1 serving: 267 cal., 8g fat (5g sat. fat), 22mg chol., 428mg sod., 46g carb. (26g sugars, 2g fiber), 3g pro.

PERFECT PEPPERMINT PATTIES

I make lots of different candy at Christmas to give as gifts. It can be time-consuming, but it's worth it to see the delight it brings people. Calling for just a few ingredients, this candy is one that is quite simple to prepare.

—*Joanne Adams, Bath, ME*

PREP: 20 MIN. + CHILLING • **MAKES:** 5 DOZEN

3¾ cups confectioners' sugar
3 Tbsp. butter, softened
2 to 3 tsp. peppermint extract
½ tsp. vanilla extract
¼ cup evaporated milk
2 cups semisweet chocolate chips
2 Tbsp. shortening

1. In a large bowl, combine the first 4 ingredients. Add milk and mix well. Roll into 1-in. balls and place on a waxed paper-lined baking sheet. Flatten with a glass to ¼-in. thickness. Cover and freeze for 30 minutes.
2. Microwave chocolate chips and shortening on high until melted; stir until smooth. Dip patties, allowing excess to drip off. Place on waxed paper; let stand until set.

1 patty: 67 cal., 3g fat (1g sat. fat), 2mg chol., 7mg sod., 11g carb. (10g sugars, 0 fiber), 0 pro.

INSPIRED BY YORK PEPPERMINT PATTIES®

YORK PEPPERMINT PATTIES

COPYCAT BERGER COOKIES

After a friend who recently traveled to Baltimore sent me a package of Berger cookies,
I was hooked. They disappeared so quickly, I decided to try to re-create them at home.
After many tests and tweaks, my husband and I gained 6 pounds between the two of us,
but it was worth it—I landed on a reproduction of the famous cookie I'm so proud of.

—Marina Castle-Kelley, Canyon Country, CA

PREP: 15 MIN. • **BAKE:** 10 MIN./BATCH + COOLING • **MAKES:** 35 COOKIES

1 cup unsalted butter, softened
1 Tbsp. baking powder
1½ tsp. salt
2 tsp. vanilla extract
1½ cups sugar
3 large eggs, room temperature
4½ cups all-purpose flour
1 cup sour cream

CHOCOLATE ICING

4 Tbsp. unsalted butter
3½ cups semisweet chocolate chips
4 oz. unsweetened chocolate, chopped
2 Tbsp. light corn syrup
1½ cups sour cream

1. Preheat oven to 400°. Beat butter, baking powder, salt and vanilla until combined. Add sugar; beat until light and fluffy, 5-7 minutes. Add eggs, 1 at a time, beating well after each addition. Add flour alternately with sour cream, beginning and ending with flour; do not overmix.
2. Drop by 3 tablespoonfuls onto greased baking sheets. With wet fingers, flatten each into a 3-in. circle.
3. Bake 10 minutes or until edges start to brown. Cool on pan 5 minutes; remove to wire racks to cool completely.
4. In a small saucepan, stir icing ingredients over low heat just until chocolate melts and mixture is smooth. Remove from heat; cool to room temperature. Using a hand mixer, beat on high until mixture thickens and becomes lighter in color, 6-7 minutes.
5. Spread 2 Tbsp. icing over flat side of each cookie; let stand until set. Store in an airtight container in the refrigerator.

1 cookie: 296 cal., 17g fat (10g sat. fat), 37mg chol., 159mg sod., 34g carb. (19g sugars, 2g fiber), 4g pro.

COPY THAT!

To test cookie doneness, use a spatula and gently lift the edge of a cookie. The top will not be brown but the edge will be slightly brown.

INSPIRED BY
BERGER'S BAKERY®
BERGER COOKIES

RECIPE INDEX